East Timor: Genocide in Paradise

Matthew Jardine

Introduction by Noam Chomsky

Odonian Press
Tucson, Arizona

Additional copies of this and other Real Story books are available from Odonian Press, Box 32375, Tucson AZ 85751 (for more on ordering our other titles, see the inside back cover). To order by credit card, or for information on quantity discounts, please write, call us at 520 296 4056 or 800 REAL STORY, or fax us at 520 296 0936.

Distribution to the book trade is through Publishers Group West, Box 8843, Emeryville CA 94662, 510 658 3453 (toll-free: 800 788 3123).

Reorganization and editing: Sandy Niemann

Final reorganization and editing: Arthur Naiman

Copyediting and proofreading: Susan McCallister

Index: Steve Rath   Cover photograph: Elaine Brière

Design and page layout: Arthur Naiman

Series editor: Arthur Naiman

Jardine, Matthew
    East Timor : genocide in paradise / Matthew Jardine.
        p.   cm.
    Includes bibliographical references and index.
    ISBN 1-878825-20-8
    1. Timor Timur (Indonesia)—Politics and government. 2. Timor Timur (Indonesia)—History—Autonomy and independence movements. 3. Political atrocities—Indonesia—Timor Timur I. Title.
DS646.59.T55J38 1995
959.8'6—dc20   95-31563
                                         CIP

Printed in the USA   Second printing—November, 1995

Odonian Press gets its name from Ursula Le Guin's wonderful novel *The Dispossessed* (though we have no connection with Ms. Le Guin or any of her publishers). The last story in her collection *The Wind's Twelve Quarters* also features the Odonians.

Odonian Press donates at least 10% of its aftertax income to organizations working for social justice.

Contents

Dedicated to Tilson and all the other children of East Timor and Indonesia. May they someday know a world of peace and justice.

Acknowledgments

There are many people to whose work and assistance I owe a great debt and who have made this project possible. Given the limits of space and—more significantly—of my memory, there are surely many that I neglect. I am appreciative nonetheless.

I would like to thank Elaine Brière, Carmel Budiardjo, Roger Clark, James Dunn, Carol and Ping Ferry, Gerry Hale, Bruno Kahn, Liem Soei Liong, John Miller, Constancio Pinto, Sharon Scharfe, Charlie Scheiner, David Webster and friends from the CNRM for all their support and assistance.

I am very grateful to Martin Ang, Allan Nairn and Mark Salzer for having read early drafts of the book, and for their critical and helpful comments. I also want to extend my gratitude to Sandy Niemann for her careful editing and patience, and to Arthur Naiman for publishing this book. In addition, I want to thank Mizue for her love and patience, and my parents for their infinite support.

Finally, I want to thank all those of East Timor and Indonesia who continue to struggle for basic human rights, human dignity and democracy. Your example inspires me and countless others throughout the world to work to claim our own humanity.

Matthew Jardine

Preface

The island of Timor lies about four hundred miles northwest of Australia and about a thousand miles due south of the southern tip of the Philippines. It's slightly larger than the state of Maryland, and most of its terrain is mountainous.

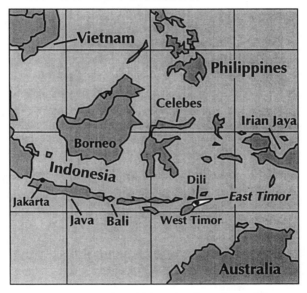

From the early 1600s, the Dutch and Portuguese fought over Timor. They ended up dividing it, with the Dutch controlling the western half and the Portuguese the eastern half.

When the Dutch East Indies won their independence and became the Republic of Indonesia in 1950, West Timor was incorporated into it. East Timor remained a Portuguese colony until the mid-1970s, when Portugal's overseas empire began to fall apart.

East Timor declared its independence on November 28, 1975. But it didn't stay independent for long. Unfortunately for the tiny nation's dreams of freedom, Indonesia controlled not only West Timor but virtually every other nearby island as well.

Most Americans don't realize how large Indonesia is. Close to 200 million people live on its 17,000 islands; only China, India and the US have larger populations. (The capital, Jakarta, is on the island of Java, where about three-fifths of Indonesia's population lives.)

Indonesia's army and government are among the most brutal in the world. In 1965, the army murdered more than a million alleged enemies of the government (including women and children) in a period of a few months.

The generals who run Indonesia aren't interested in self-determination, human rights or other wimpy, democratic ideals. They're interested in maintaining control over their vast territory and plundering it for as much profit as they can—almost always with the help of Western or Japanese partners.

Just nine days after East Timor declared its independence—and just two days after President Suharto of Indonesia hosted US President Gerald Ford and Secretary of State Henry Kissinger at a state dinner—Indonesia invaded East Timor. It was December 7, 1975 and—like the attack on Pearl Harbor on the same date in 1941—it's a day that will live in infamy.

In the first few weeks of the invasion, Indonesian troops killed tens of thousands of people. That wasn't surprising, given Indonesia's record. But the genocidal war of occupation Indonesia has been waging ever since has broken new ground, even for them.

In 1975, East Timor had a population of about 690,000. In the twenty years since then, more than 200,000 East Timorese have died as a result of the Indonesian occupation.

In this book, Matthew Jardine and Noam Chomsky tell the story of East Timor's heroic resistance against all odds. They also explain why you hardly ever hear about East Timor on TV or in the newspapers—and why, when the Indonesian army murders someone there, you and I pay for the bullets they use.

Arthur Naiman

Introduction

Noam Chomsky

In the annals of crime of this terrible century, Indonesia's assault against East Timor ranks high, not only because of its scale—perhaps the greatest death toll relative to the population since the Holocaust—but because it would have been so easy to prevent, and to bring to an end at any time. There is no need for threats to bomb Jakarta, or even to impose sanctions on the aggressor. It would suffice for the great powers to refrain from their eager participation in Indonesia's crimes—to stop putting guns into the hands of the killers and torturers while joining them in robbery of the off-shore oil of the Timor Gap.

Two years ago, Indonesian Foreign Minister Ali Alatas said that his government faced an important choice on East Timor, which had become "like a sharp piece of gravel in our shoes." Benedict Anderson, a leading specialist on Indonesia, took this to be one of many signs of second thoughts: "Alatas doesn't spell out what the choice is," Anderson commented, "but he's implying you should take your shoe off and get rid of the gravel."

The gravel was not sharpened by Western power. Quite the contrary: the West and Japan have been willing partners in Indonesia's conquest and annexation of the former Portuguese colony. Well before Indonesia began its campaign of sub-version and terror in 1975, followed by direct invasion on December 7, the British Embassy in Jakarta reported that, "Certainly as seen from here, it is in Britain's interest that Indonesia should absorb the territory as soon as and as unobtrusively as possible; and that if it comes to the crunch and there is a row in the United Nations, we should keep our heads down and avoid siding against the Indonesian government."

Australia shared this judgment. In August 1975, Ambassador to Jakarta Richard Woolcott advised in secret cables that Australia take "a prag-matic rather than a principled stand" with regard to the forthcoming invasion because "that is what national interest and foreign policy is all about." Along with the ritual reference to "the Australian defence interest," Woolcott suggested that a favorable treaty on the Timor Gap "could be much more readily negotiated with Indonesia...than with Portugal or independent Portuguese Timor." He recommended a preference for "Kissingerian realism" over "Wilsonian idealism"—a distinction that can perhaps be detected in actual practice, with a powerful enough microscope.

The reasons for support for Indonesia's crimes went well beyond oil and "defence interests," including control of a deep-water passage for nuclear submarines. Indonesia has been an honored ally ever since General Suharto came to power in 1965 with a "boiling bloodbath" that was "the West's best news for years in Asia" *(Time)*, a "staggering mass slaughter of Communists and pro-Communists," mostly landless peasants, that provided a "gleam of light in Asia" *(New York Times)*.

Euphoria knew no bounds, along with praise for the "Indonesian moderates" who prevailed *(New York Times)* and their leader, who is "at heart benign" *(The Economist)*. Not only did the welcome bloodbath destroy the only mass-based political party in Indonesia, but it opened the rich resources of the country to Western exploitation and even justified the American war in Vietnam, which "provided a shield for the sharp reversal of Indonesia's shift toward Communism," as Freedom House soberly explained with no reservations. Such favors are not quickly forgotten.

Woolcott offered some illustrations of "Kissingerian realism." Noting with diplomatic understatement that "the United States might have some influence on Indonesia at present," he reported that Kissinger had instructed US Ambassador David Newsom to avoid the Timor issue and cut down Embassy reporting, allowing "events to take their course." Newsom informed Woolcott that if Indonesia were to invade, the US hoped it would do so "effectively, quickly, and not use our equipment"—90% of its weapons supply.

Another lesson in realism was given by UN Ambassador Daniel Patrick Moynihan, celebrated for his courageous defense of international law and human rights. "The United States wished things to turn out as they did," he writes in his memoirs, "and worked to bring this about. The Department of State desired that the United Nations prove utterly ineffective in whatever measures it undertook. This task was given me, and I carried it forward with no inconsiderable success." Moynihan cites figures of 60,000 killed in the first few months, "almost the proportion of casualties experienced by the Soviet Union during the Second World War," a foretaste of still greater successes soon to come.

Western governments were fully aware of what was happening throughout, contrary to subsequent pretense. As revealed in leaked internal records, Kissinger's worst fear was that his complicity in the aggression might become public, and "used against me" by real or imagined political enemies. Cable traffic shows that after "Suharto was given the green light," the main concern of the Embassy and State Department was "about the problems that would be created for us if the public and Congress became aware" of the American role, according to Philip Liechty, then a senior CIA officer in Jakarta.

Weapons provided by the US were limited strictly to self-defense. That posed no problem for Kissingerian realism: "And we can't construe a Communist government in the middle of Indonesia as self-defense?," Kissinger asked with derision when the question was raised in internal discussion. An independent East Timor would be "Communist" by the usual criteria: it might not follow orders in a sprightly enough manner, interfering with the "national interest." New arms were sent, including counterinsurgency equipment; "everything that you need to fight a major war against somebody who doesn't have any guns," Liechty comments, adding that the advanced military equipment proved decisive, as other sources confirm.

Had there been a challenge, ample precedent could have been cited. "Great souls care little for small morals," another statesman observed two centuries ago.

By 1977, Indonesia found itself short of weapons, an indication of the scale of its attack. The Carter administration accelerated the arms flow. Britain joined in as atrocities peaked in 1978, while France announced that it would sell arms to Indonesia and protect it from any public "embarrassment." Others too sought to gain what profit they could from the slaughter and torture of Timorese.

The press added its contribution. Coverage of East Timor in the United States had been high in 1974–75, amidst concerns over the break-up of the Portuguese empire. As another "boiling blood-bath" proceeded, coverage declined, keeping largely to the lies and apologetics of the State Department and Indonesian generals. By 1978, as the slaughter reached genocidal levels, coverage reached flat zero. The same was true in Canada, another leading supporter of Indonesia.

In 1990, the issue of Timor received some attention when Iraq invaded Kuwait, eliciting a response from the West rather unlike its reaction to Indonesia's vastly more bloody invasion and annexation of a small oil-rich country next door. Much ingenuity was displayed in explaining that the distinction did not lie in the locus of power and profit, but in some more subtle quality that preserves Anglo-American virtue. Similar gyrations had been undertaken a decade earlier to justify the radically different reaction to simultaneous atrocities in Cambodia and Timor; crucially different, to be sure, in that the latter could have been readily terminated.

Some commentators were forthright. Australian Foreign Minister Gareth Evans explained in 1990 that "the world is a pretty unfair place, littered with examples of acquisition by force." Since "there is no binding legal obligation not to recognize the acquisition of territory that was acquired by force," Australia may proceed to share Timor's oil with the conqueror. The dispensation would presumably not have extended to a Libya-Iraq treaty on Kuwait oil. Meanwhile Prime Minister Hawke declared that "big countries cannot invade small neighbors and get away with it" (referring to Iraq and Kuwait); "would-be aggressors will think twice before invading smaller neighbors," secure in the lesson that "the rule of law must prevail over the rule of force in international relations"—at least, when the "national interest" so dictates.

The Timor issue reached threshold again in November 1991, when Indonesian troops attacked a graveyard commemoration of an earlier assassination, massacring hundreds of people and severely beating two US reporters. The tactical error called for the standard cover-up, deemed satisfactory by Western leaders. Oil exploration proceeded on course, contracts with Australian, British, Japanese, Dutch and American companies were reported in the six months following the massacre. "To the capitalist governors," a Timorese priest wrote, "Timor's petroleum smells better than Timorese blood and tears."

The primary reason why Indonesia might consider "taking the shoe off" is given in the final words of the powerful and revealing chapters on Timor in the 1994 edition of John Pilger's *Distant Voices*. The reason is "the enduring heroism of the people of East Timor, who continue to resist invaders even as the crosses multiply on the hillsides," a constant "reminder of the fallibility of brute power and of the cynicism of others."

However courageous they may be, the people of East Timor have no hope without outside support. No amount of courage and unity will prevent Indonesian transmigration, atrocities and destruction of the indigenous culture, funded and supported by the great powers.

Though the pace has been glacial, support for Timorese rights has finally reached a significant level in the United States. The truth began to seep into the public domain, compelling the media to take some notice and raising impediments to the "pragmatic course."

A headline in the *Boston Globe* on the anniversary of the 1991 massacre reads: "Indonesian general, facing suit, flees Boston." Sent to study at Harvard after the massacre, the general was charged in a suit on behalf of a woman whose son was among those murdered in the graveyard—many more afterwards, as revealed by Pilger and the courageous Indonesian academic George Aditjondro, who released investigations based on 20 years research that supports the most gruesome estimates of atrocities. Popular awareness and activism have become strong enough so that favored mass murders can no longer find a comfortable refuge in the United States, as had been learned a year earlier by one of Guatemala's leading killers, General Hector Gramajo, in a similar manner.

Congress has imposed barriers on military aid and training, which the White House has had to evade in ever more devious ways, particularly in recent months. Sensing the opportunity, Britain moved effectively under Thatcher's guiding hand to take first place in the highly profitable enterprise of war crimes. As explained by Defense Procurement Minister Alan Clark, "I don't really fill my mind much with what one set of foreigners is doing to another" when there is money to be made by arms sales. We must insist on "reserving the right to bomb niggers," as Lloyd George recognized 60 years ago.

John Pilger's recent work, including the remarkable documentary based on his visit to East Timor, threatens to arouse the Western public to a heightened awareness of what is being perpetrated in their names. Its great significance is attested by the angry response it has evoked from high government officials. To draw aside the veils of deceit that conceal the real world is no small achievement. But it will join other failed efforts unless the public response goes beyond mere awareness, to actions to end shameful complicity in crime.

Noam Chomsky
Originally published in The Guardian *(London), 7/5/94*

The Santa Cruz massacre

On November 12, 1991, a crowd of mourners gathered at a local parish church in East Timor's capital, Dili. They'd come to attend a memorial mass for Sebastiao Gomes, a pro-independence activist who had been killed at that same church by Indonesian soldiers two weeks earlier.

Such killings had become common occurrences since the Indonesian invasion. But this particular day of mourning would have special significance—in large part because journalists from the US and Great Britain were there to report it.

When the mass ended, a procession began to the Santa Cruz Cemetery, about a mile away. Although Indonesian soldiers lined the streets, the mourners unfurled banners and shouted pro-independence slogans. This uncharacteristically open defiance of Indonesian authority caught the attention of those whose homes and places of work lined the procession route. Supporters joined in, and soon the crowd had swelled to thousands.

At the cemetery, some of the crowd went to the gravesite with Sebastiao's family. Others waited outside the walls. They were the first to notice that Indonesian army trucks had blocked the road back to town, and that a column of armed soldiers was slowly making its way toward the crowd.

Eyewitness Allan Nairn of the *New Yorker* reports what happened next. Without warning, and without provocation, "soldiers raised their rifles, and took aim. Then, acting in unison, they opened fire....Men and women fell, shivering, in the street, rolling from the impact of the bullets. Some were backpedalling, and tripping, their hands held up. Others simply tried to turn and run. The soldiers jumped over fallen bodies and fired at the people still upright. They chased down young boys and girls and shot them in the back." When it was over, more than 250 people had been killed and hundreds more wounded. (The soldiers also badly beat Nairn and fellow US journalist Amy Goodman.)

Max Stahl, a British journalist whose video camera captured the horror, called it a "cold-blooded and premeditated massacre." Eyewitnesses told him that Indonesian soldiers killed many of the wounded at the military hospital in Dili; they "crushed the skulls of the wounded with large rocks, ran over them with trucks, stabbed them and administered—with doctors present—poisonous disinfecting chemicals as medicines." Stahl estimates that 50–200 of the wounded died in this way.

When news of the Santa Cruz massacre appeared in the Western media, it sparked international outrage. The US Congress and European Parliament passed resolutions condemning Indonesia, and the Netherlands, Denmark and Canada suspended aid. Editorials favoring East Timorese self-determination appeared in newspapers throughout the West.

Indonesia moved swiftly to stifle the criticism. It expressed official "regret" for what had happened, set up an official investigation of the incident, relieved the two top military commanders for East Timor (sending them abroad for "study") and sentenced a few low-ranking officers for ostensibly disobeying orders. It also sent its foreign minister on a tour of the US, Canada and Western Europe to repair Indonesia's damaged reputation (demonstrations plagued him wherever he went).

But the words of two top-ranking military officials undoubtedly expressed Jakarta's real sentiments. General Try Sutrisno, the commander of the Indonesian military at the time of the massacre and now the country's vice-president, said that the East Timorese who'd gathered at the cemetery were "disrupters" who "must be crushed." He added, "Delinquents like these have to be shot, and we will shoot them."

General Mantriri, regional commander for East Timor just after the Santa Cruz massacre, declared that the massacre was "proper" and added: "We don't regret anything." That lack of regret was clear from the sentences meted out to participants in the Santa Cruz march and to East Timorese demonstrators in Jakarta who protested the massacre. They ranged from five years to life imprisonment.

Despite the media coverage the Santa Cruz massacre received in the West, you can still go months without hearing a word about East Timor and the people who are dying there.

Portuguese rule

East Timor, under the Portuguese, seemed to sit still in history. The clock of development didn't tick there.   José Ramos-Horta

Portuguese traders arrived on Timor around 1515, anxious to take advantage of the island's already lucrative sandalwood trade.Timorese leaders on the coast exchanged sandalwood brought from the mountainous interior for Portuguese guns, cloth and iron tools.

In the beginning, these Portuguese visits had little effect on the Timorese. Most of the islanders lived in small, relatively isolated villages in the interior, where subsistence agriculture and animist religions predominated.

Eventually, however, the European influence became more invasive. In the late 1500s, Dominican friars from Portugal established a mission in the major sandalwood port. Not long after that, the *Topasses,* or Black Portuguese—the offspring of Portuguese soldiers, sailors and traders and women from neighboring islands—began to settle on Timor. They spread Portuguese culture and influence, and soon controlled the local trading networks.

Soon afterwards, the Dutch began visiting Timor, to obtain sandalwood and slaves. The two colonial powers were soon in conflict, as each tried to extend its influence on the island. The next two centuries were dominated by power struggles between the colonial powers, the *Topasses* and indigenous Timorese. The official division of the island into West (Dutch) Timor and East (Portuguese) Timor wasn't formalized until 1913.

In the first 300 years of colonial rule, Portugal showed less interest in East Timor than in any of its other colonies. In the 1860s, Alfred R. Wallace, a British explorer, described the situation like this:

> The Portuguese government in Timor is a most miserable one. Nobody seems to care the least about the improvement of the country, and at this time, after three hundred years of occupation, there has not been a mile of road made beyond the town [Dili], and there is not a solitary European residence in the interior.

But by the end of the 19th century, this situation began to change rapidly. Portugal wanted to boost its economic power to catch up with its European rivals and to stave off threats to its colonies from Britain, Germany and France, who were looking to expand their empires.

Hoping that the colonies themselves could become a significant source of income for the mother country, Portugal began to increase the economic and social development of East Timor. This often entailed heavy-handed tactics like the forced cultivation of cash crops, forced labor to build the territory's infrastructure, and the levying of head taxes.

Such methods led to widespread resentment and finally large-scale violence, culminating in an uprising that began in 1910, led by a local ruler. By 1912, the rebellion threatened Portuguese control of Dili itself, but it was violently suppressed with the aid of African troops from the Portuguese colony of Mozambique.

At the same time, the Portuguese administration began cultivating a town-based elite of native East Timorese in order to fill the new administrative, managerial and service-oriented jobs that were being generated by development. These jobs required both education and a colonial perspective, and the Catholic Church helped cultivate both. By 1900, it was running twenty schools that emphasized Portuguese language, geography and culture.

Despite these development efforts, Timor never became much of an economic asset to Portugal. In fact, it remained one of the most economically backward colonies in all of Southeast Asia. As one historian described it:

> On the eve of World War II the capital, Dili, had no electricity and no town water supply; there were no paved roads, no telephone services (other than to the houses and offices of senior officials), and not even a wharf for cargo handling.

World War II was to bring even the modest efforts Portugal was making to modernize East Timor to an abrupt standstill.

World War II and after

When the Western allies declared war against Japan, they decided to use the island of Timor as a line of defense against Japan's southward advance (despite protests from the neutral Portuguese). By mid-December 1941, just ten days after Pearl Harbor, about 400 Dutch East Indies and Australian troops landed west of Dili.

Two months later, Japan attacked the island, and quickly drove the Dutch out of the western half. In East Timor, a few hundred Australian commandos and some Timorese managed to hold about 20,000 Japanese soldiers at bay for almost a year. But by January 1943, the Japanese controlled the entire island.

The Japanese occupation was one of the darkest times in East Timor's history (though its cruelty and devastation has been surpassed by the Indonesians). Here's how Iwamura Shouachi, who commanded a Japanese platoon in East Timor for over two years, described the hardships the Japanese military imposed:

> It is painful to speak today of the sacrifices and burdens we forced upon the East Timorese.... We ordered chiefs to mobilize people *en masse* for road construction...to work without receiving food or compensation. Because of food shortage [sic] people died of starvation every day. Food for Japanese soldiers and horses to transport ammunition were confiscated from the people, and some of the troops under my command raped Timorese women.

Had the Australians and the Allies left the island alone, the Japanese might very well have ignored Timor, or at most sent a token contingent of soldiers. But instead, about 60,000 East Timorese lost their lives as a result of the brutal Japanese occupation and the Allied bombing that aimed to dislodge it. The war badly damaged Dili and partly destroyed many of the territory's principal towns and villages.

With Japan's defeat in August 1945, Portugal returned and reasserted its control over East Timor, which gradually returned to its pre-war state. The Portuguese began to rebuild the devastated colonial infrastructure, often employing the same brutal methods and forced labor they'd used before the war.

With the exception of a serious revolt in 1959 (which was quickly put down), relations between the Timorese and the Portuguese remained fairly calm—though resentment simmered beneath the surface. The Catholic Church, whose membership had swelled because of the harrowing experiences of the war, helped smooth tensions by encouraging pro-Portuguese sentiment in worship and education.

Throughout Southeast Asia, the post-war era was one of great political upheaval, as colonized territories sought independence and as returning colonial powers tried to reassert their control. The people of the Dutch East Indies declared Indonesia to be a free country on August 17, 1945, while still under Japanese occupation.

When the Dutch returned, they refused to recognize this declaration of independence and instead waged a brutal military campaign to reclaim their colony. But by the end of 1949, massive resistance forced the Dutch to recognize the independence of Indonesia. The US government pressured the Dutch to do this, since it believed that a stable, independent Indonesia would provide a better business environment for US capital than a rebellious, war-torn colony.

In East Timor itself, post-war nationalism came more slowly, but it finally did come. By the late 1950s, public radio began broadcasting in Portuguese, Tetum (the *lingua franca* used by people who spoke different native languages) and Chinese (business in the colony was dominated by ethnic Chinese—i.e. people of Chinese ancestry born in East Timor). A government-controlled newspaper, *A Voz de Timor,* began publishing in 1960. Since they were regularly censored by authorities, however, these sources offered only limited exposure to "foreign" ideas.

Certain elements in the Catholic Church played an important role in facilitating nationalistic thinking. Although most Catholic schools focussed on things Portuguese, the Jesuits were often critical of colonialism and of social conditions. In their seminary outside Dili, where many of the East Timorese who worked for the Portuguese administration received their education, Jesuit teachers discussed burgeoning nationalist movements and progressive approaches to Third World development, and promoted a sense of Timorese identity among their students.

A church newspaper, *Seara,* which was free from censorship laws, taught Tetum to its readers and sometimes served as a lively forum for progressive ideas. Some of its contributors, who'd had contact with African liberation movements, began to privately advocate East Timor's independence. The Portuguese authorities forced *Seara* to stop publication in 1973, but by that time like-minded dissidents were already meeting clandestinely with one another in Dili.

Although the vast majority of the population still lived as they had for centuries in rural hamlets, a small, educated elite had developed by the 1970s. When the Portuguese empire finally began to crumble, this group of students, teachers and even colonial administrators helped tiny East Timor emerge from its relative isolation into the turbulent world of international power politics.

The struggle for independence

Don't dream about having...a state of Timtim [the Indonesian name for East Timor]. There is no such thing!....From now on, Timtim is the same as other regions. So don't try to be latter day heroes, beating your breasts and proclaiming, 'I am a Timtim patriot.' There is no such thing as a Timtim nation, there is only an Indonesian nation....

If you try to make your own state...it will be crushed by [the Indonesian military]....There have been bigger rebellions, there have been greater differences of opinion with the government than the small number calling themselves Fretilin, or whoever their sympathizers are here. We will crush them all! I repeat, we will crush them all!

Indonesian Defense Minister Benny Murdani,
speaking in Dili, February 1990

In late April 1974, a group of left-leaning military officers stationed in Lisbon (Portugal's capital) overthrew the country's fascist government in a relatively bloodless coup. There was some disagreement among the officers (who called themselves the Armed Forces Movement, or MFA) about what to do with Portugal's colonies. The conservative head of the MFA favored what he called "progressive autonomy...within a Portuguese framework," but other officers, many of whom had recently returned from fighting liberation movements in the African colonies, championed "some form of independence."

In June 1974, Portugal laid out three possible options for East Timor: continued association with Portugal, independence, or becoming part of Indonesia. But the Portuguese government took no immediate action on any of these options.

In East Timor itself, however, the response to the coup was much less sluggish. Within little more than a month, three political parties had formed: the UDT, the ASDT (which later became FRETILIN) and APODETI.

The first party founded, the UDT (the Timorese Democratic Union), was generally conservative and pro-Portuguese. It initially advocated continued ties with Lisbon, but as opposition to colonialism mounted, it soon began supporting the idea of eventual total independence.

The second party founded, the ASDT (the Association of Timorese Social Democrats), advocated "the universal doctrines of socialism and democracy." Fully committed to independence from the beginning, it envisioned an eight-to-ten-year decolonization period in which the East

Timorese could develop the political and economic structures necessary for independence.

Both the UDT and the ASDT drew their leadership largely from the middle and upper classes—Timorese who had studied at the Jesuit college at Soibada and the seminary outside of Dili, and who were colonial administrators or school teachers. East Timor's wealthiest citizens tended to support the UDT. They included senior administrative officials, native leaders and prominent plantation owners. One UDT leader—its first president, in fact—was later appointed governor of East Timor by the Indonesians, a post he held from 1981 to 1992.

The third party, APODETI (the Timorese Popular Democratic Association) favored an "autonomous integration" with Indonesia. (Its original name—the Association for the Integration of Timor into Indonesia—was quickly changed for public-relations purposes.)

APODETI, which never had more than a few hundred members, appears to have been largely a project of the Indonesian military's intelligence service. The last thing Indonesia wanted was another independent country on its border, and it was dedicated to making sure this never happened.

Three men who'd been cooperating with the Indonesian military for a number of years became key leaders in APODETI. And immediately after APODETI's founding, Indonesia began providing East Timorese agents with financial support.

UDT began as the largest and most popular group, but it soon began to lose ground to the ASDT, which was better organized and more innovative. When the deputy president of the Indonesian parliament said that he favored Indonesian control of East Timor, the ASDT sent an envoy, José Ramos-Horta, to Jakarta, where he was assured by Indonesia's foreign minister that Indonesia unequivocally supported East Timorese self-determination.

Next José Ramos-Horta went to Australia, but the Australian government was unwilling to meet with him or to make any official statement in favor of self-determination for East Timor. He did, however, get support from church groups, trade unionists, academics and members of parliament.

As its members—and the East Timorese population in general—became more radical, ASDT changed its name, in September 1974, to FRETILIN (the Revolutionary Front for an Independent East Timor) and demanded immediate independence from Portugal. FRETILIN volunteers began to move out from Dili into the rural areas, teaching villagers to read and write Tetum, establishing agricultural cooperatives, helping organize labor unions and other groups, and promoting local culture by encouraging the creation of nationalist poems, songs and dances. Thanks to these activities, FRETILIN became, by early 1975, the most popular of the three parties.

While Portugal's president called full East Timorese independence "unrealistic," the MFA's new governor of East Timor (and local MFA officers there) wanted to help the country gain its freedom. In December 1974, they invited the three parties to advise Lisbon on how to decolonize East Timor. The UDT and FRETILIN joined in the process and then formed a coalition. APODETI refused to participate, claiming it recognized only the Indonesian government, not the Portuguese.

In May 1975, the UDT, FRETILIN and the MFA agreed that a transitional government would be set up by October, and that elections for a national constituent assembly would be held in the fall of 1976. But Indonesia had different plans. By mid-1974, it had developed Operation Komodo—named after the Komodo dragons, giant man-eating lizards that live on other Indonesian islands.

Operation Komodo aimed to strengthen APODETI and weaken FRETILIN, and it scored a number of diplomatic successes. Meeting with Indonesian President Suharto in September 1974, Australian Prime Minister Gough Whitlam stated that an independent East Timor would be "unviable" and "a potential threat to the area." He voiced his support for a voluntary union between East Timor and Indonesia. Although he added that Australia wouldn't approve of the use of force in East Timor, his comments overall were seen by Jakarta as being very favorable to their position.

When FRETILIN and the UDT started to work together, Indonesia stepped up Operation Komodo. In mid-February 1975, the Indonesian military (commonly referred to by the acronym ABRI) staged exercises in Sumatra that simulated an air and sea attack on East Timor. Soon thereafter, Indonesia began disseminating false reports of a planned coup by the MFA and FRETILIN, and of supposed persecution of APODETI members.

Operation Komodo, combined with FRETILIN's growing popularity, weakened the UDT-FRETILIN coalition. Indonesia was able to convince the more conservative members of the UDT that international isolation would result if leftists were allowed to remain in the coalition. In late May 1975, the UDT formally withdrew from the coalition.

UDT leaders met with Indonesian officials in Jakarta and became convinced that Indonesia wouldn't allow East Timorese independence under FRETILIN and probably not even under the UDT. They felt that only by purging the territory of "communist" influence would they have any chance of preventing an Indonesian invasion.

Finally, in mid-August 1975, Indonesia gave the UDT false intelligence reports of an imminent FRETILIN power grab, complete with clandestine Chinese arms shipments and "Vietnamese terrorists" entering East Timor to help FRETILIN. The UDT launched a coup, quickly capturing the communications station and the airport in Dili.

But the UDT greatly underestimated the strength of FRETILIN, which was able to persuade most East Timorese units in the Portuguese army to side with it. Soon FRETILIN controlled all of Dili and by late September it had driven 500 UDT soldiers and 2500 refugees (mostly family of UDT leaders and soldiers) into West Timor. The brief civil war was over.

(Indonesia permitted the refugees to enter West Timor only if they signed a petition calling for East Timor's integration into Indonesia. As a former UDT leader put it: "It was the last thing we wanted, but with FRETILIN forces closing in on us and without food, we really had no alternative but to agree.")

FRETILIN immediately began to set up a *de facto* government to fill in for the Portuguese, who had fled during the civil war. The former Australian Consul in Dili, James Dunn, described the people's response:

> This administrative structure had obvious short-comings, but it clearly enjoyed widespread support or cooperation from the population, including many former UDT supporters....
> Indeed, the leaders of the victorious party were welcomed warmly and spontaneously in all main centers by crowds of Timorese. In my long association with the territory, I had never before witnessed such demonstrations of spontaneous warmth and support from the ordinary people.

In order to complete the process of decolonization, FRETILIN called for a peace conference between it, Portugal and Indonesia, but Portugal's constant postponements prevented the talks from ever materializing. Meanwhile, ABRI (the Indonesian military) was making incursions over the border from West Timor, to give the appearance of an ongoing civil war. (Indonesia denied these incursions, but even the CIA confirmed them.)

ABRI soon captured some towns near the border between East and West Timor. Their campaign culminated in a two-week land, air and sea attack on a town called Atabae, just 35 miles from Dili. ABRI finally took Atabae on November 28th, 1975. Faced with an imminent, full-scale invasion, FRETILIN declared the independence of the Democratic Republic of East Timor that same day.

FRETILIN hoped this declaration would give East Timor some international protection, but

only four former Portuguese colonies in Africa recognized the new country immediately. Western
nations, which knew all about Indonesia's plans to
invade, remained silent.

Indonesia invades

*The Indonesian forces are killing indiscriminate-
ly. Women and children are being shot in the
streets. We are all going to be killed. I repeat,
we are all going to be killed....This is an appeal
for international help. Please do something to
stop this invasion.*

FRETILIN radio broadcast from Dili
in the early hours of December 7, 1975

*The total may be 50,000, but what does this
mean if compared with 600,000 people who
want to join Indonesia? Then what is the big
fuss? It is possible that they may have been
killed by Australians and not us. Who knows?
It was war.*

Indonesia's foreign minister, Adam Malik,
referring to the number of East Timorese killed
in the first fifteen months of the "civil war"

On December 7, 1975, the long-feared invasion
began. At 2 am, Indonesian ships began to bom-
bard the outskirts of Dili, where they thought
FRETILIN's military wing, FALINTIL, had artillery
batteries. By 5 am, planes were dropping para-
troopers into the waterfront area.

ABRI soldiers began to rampage through the
town. According to the former Catholic bishop of
Dili, "The soldiers who landed started killing

everyone they could find. There were many dead bodies in the streets—all we could see were the soldiers killing, killing, killing."

Eloise, an East Timorese living in Dili, awoke to the sounds of invading troops. She describes the atrocities that followed:

On 7 December we woke and heard this big noise of planes and saw parachutes and planes covering the light—it became dark because of them, so many. Then there were shots and we went inside and kept listening to more and more shooting. In the afternoon some Timorese came and told us everyone must come to surrender at headquarters....

Once we got there they divided us: the women and children and old men to one side, and on the other young boys [and men]....

Then an Indonesian screams an order and we hear machine guns running through the men. We see the boys and men dying right there. Some see their husbands die. We look at each other stunned. We think they are going to kill us next. All of us just turn and pick up the children and babies and run screaming, wild, everywhere....

[Later] my sister went to look for her husband and son. On her way she met a friend crying who told her, "Don't bother going there. I have just seen my cousin being eaten by a dog. They are all dead. Only the dogs are alive there.

Mr. Siong, a Chinese Timorese living near the harbor, reported similar atrocities:

At midday [on December 7] they take six of us [men] to work at the harbour....[where] we have to pick up...dead bodies....There were a lot of iron pipes on the wharf and we must tie the dead bodies on to them with parachute rope and throw them into the sea....

[Chinese Timorese from a Dili suburb] came in groups of two or three or four, stood on the wharf and were shot. One group after the other coming and coming, killed and thrown in the sea. Two were couples, one with young children who went with relatives. The other couple were elderly, and the rest were men....

Next they bring the ten [men who had been working with us]....The Indonesians tell them to stand in line and face the sea and then they are shot with a machine gun. Four people in that first sixteen of us...were father and son, but the Indonesians didn't know this. There on the wharf they kill the father, and the son must tie and throw his father into the sea. Then they kill the other son and his father is one of the six of us who must tie and throw his body.

After the initial mass killings, the soldiers began looting homes and churches, loading whatever they had stolen—furniture, cars, motorcycles and even windows—onto ships destined for Java (where most ABRI officers are based).

The ABRI troops also started looking for "girls." Olinda, a young Chinese Timorese woman reported what her uncle had seen:

After they landed in Dili the Indonesians....asked everywhere, "Where are the single girls? I want to marry," and this kind of thing. An uncle spoke Bahasa Indonesia [the official Indonesian language], for trade with West Timor. They forced him to go with them to interpret. He came back and told how the Indonesians were raping Timorese women.

Refugees reported soldiers raping women in front of their husbands or fathers, severely beating, imprisoning or sometimes even killing those men who refused to surrender their wives or daughters. Women and girls who were active in organizations linked to FRETILIN or relatives of FRETILIN members were subjected to the worst treatment. The soldiers arrested and imprisoned most of them; many were also repeatedly tortured and raped.

Many East Timorese fled to the mountains to avoid the oncoming troops. One of them, a woman called Edhina, described the situation:

> We were very frightened and ran to the bush....There were 40,000 of us, the fighters said. I had never seen so many people together....
>
> The Javanese kept attacking and dropping bombs and we were like animals running from one place to the other carrying our children, going this way and that way. We slept anywhere, in the rain, in the mud, even near the dead animals. The bombs would come and we would stand up and run again. On the way we ate anything growing, anything we could find. In the daytime we went into caves or under rocks to hide. We could come out at night to sleep in the open air and cook, make a hole and light a little fire without smoke, only coals.
>
> People and animals ran, pushed to the insides of the mountains where there was no water. In the beginning we could carry food but after a while we couldn't carry that and carry our children. We were running all the time and we were weaker. When people died we'd just lay them next to the dead animals.

In the first two days of the invasion, 2000 people in Dili were slaughtered. Of these, 500–700 were ethnic Chinese (Indonesia has a long history of anti-Chinese sentiment).

A few days after the assault on Dili, the Indonesian soldiers attacked other major towns and eventually pushed inland. On Christmas Day, the original 10,000 ABRI troops were supplemented by 15,000–20,000 more. By mid-February—a little over two months after the invasion began—60,000 East Timorese were dead.

After the invasion, Indonesia set up a puppet legislative assembly, whose 28 members—described by Indonesia as "prominent citizens of East Timor"—were handpicked by Indonesian intelligence officers, with the help of APODETI, who made sure they had no previous ties to FRETILIN or the UDT.

On May 31, 1976, this puppet assembly declared that East Timor wanted to become part of Indonesia. Observers at this event have stated that it was completely staged by the Indonesian authorities. The few journalists and junior diplomats from other countries who attended the proceedings were not permitted to speak with any delegates of the People's Assembly. As one journalist stated:

> Immediately after the council meeting, all were led back into their cars and briefly driven around the town before going straight back to the airport ....No one had a chance even to shake hands with council members, and executive members of the Provisional Government refused to answer press questions, climbing immediately into their new Volvo cars.

In July 1976, President Suharto signed into law East Timor's formal "integration" into the Unitary State of the Republic of Indonesia.

UN response to the invasion

Five days after the invasion, the United Nations General Assembly passed a resolution that deplored the invasion, called on Indonesia to withdraw immediately, and upheld the East Timorese people's right of self-determination. The vote was 72 to 10, with 43 abstentions, including the US, Canada and most Western European nations. Seven subsequent resolutions on East Timor have been passed by the General Assembly (the last one in 1982); France, Germany and Britain have abstained, and the US, Australia and Japan have voted *No,* on most of them—even when the resolution was only to instruct the Secretary General to investigate the situation.

On December 22, 1975, at Portugal's urging, the UN Security Council unanimously passed a resolution that condemned Jakarta's invasion and occupation, and supported East Timor's right to self-determination. (A similar resolution passed in April 1976, with the US and Japan abstaining.)

José Ramos-Horta, FRETILIN's UN representative at the time, explained the vote this way: "Permanent members of the Security Council [couldn't] have abstained on such a blatant case of armed aggression involving a NATO ally [Portugal]," especially since "the Security Council is a more visible body than the General Assembly." In other words, the West's affirmative vote was more an attempt to save face than a condemnation of the invasion, and the earlier vote in the General Assembly more closely represented their position.

International legal specialist Roger Clark has argued that if further and stronger Security Council resolutions had been proposed, the US would have blocked their approval. A statement by Daniel Patrick Moynihan, US ambassador to the UN during the Ford administration, bears out Clark's analysis. Concerning UN inaction on East Timor, Moynihan boasted that "The [US] Department of State desired that the United Nations prove utterly ineffective in whatever measures it undertook. This task was given to me, and I carried it forward with no inconsiderable success."

A close look at individual countries' behind-the-scenes dealings with Indonesia shows that their behavior at the UN was part of a much larger pattern of support for Indonesia. Not only did a number of powerful Western or Western-aligned countries fail to condemn the invasion; they also either knew the invasion was imminent and did nothing to prevent it, or were actually complicit in Indonesia's brutality. The most significant accomplice was the US.

US support for Indonesia

America stands as it always has, against aggression, against those who would use force to replace the rule of law.

US President George Bush, 1990,
referring to the Iraqi invasion of Kuwait

When I think of Indonesia—a country on the equator with 180 million people, a median age

> *of 18, and a Muslim ban on alcohol—I feel like
> I know what heaven looks like.*
>
> Coca-Cola President Donald R. Keough, c. 1992

It's clear that the US knew about the upcoming invasion and avoided taking any action that might have stopped it. In August 1975, Australia's ambassador to Indonesia cabled the Department of Foreign Affairs in Canberra (Australia's capital), as follows:

> The United States might have some influence on Indonesia at the present as Indonesia really wants and needs US assistance in its military re-equipment program.... But [US] Ambassador Newsom told me last night that he is under instructions from [US Secretary of State Henry] Kissinger personally not to involve himself in discussions on Timor with the Indonesians on the ground that the US is involved in enough problems of greater importance overseas at present....His present attitude is that the US should keep out of the Portuguese Timor situation and allow events to take their course.

US President Gerald Ford and Secretary of State Henry Kissinger were in Jakarta visiting Indonesian President Suharto the two days before the invasion. There's little doubt that Ford gave Suharto the green light to invade. Kissinger told reporters in Jakarta that "the US understands Indonesia's position on the question" of East Timor, and Ford said that, given a choice between East Timor and Indonesia, the US "had to be on the side of Indonesia." (US support for the invasion was important to Suharto because ABRI relied heavily on US weaponry, which US law states can only be used for defensive purposes.)

In early 1976, the US voiced its *de facto* recognition of Jakarta's annexation of East Timor. An unnamed US State Department official explained: "In terms of the bilateral relations between the US and Indonesia, we are more or less condoning the incursion into East Timor."

These US actions weren't surprising, given the history of business relations between the two countries. By the end of World War I, the US and Japan supplied almost a third of the Dutch East Indies' imports. In turn, US-based corporations located there supplied the US with tin, rubber and oil. By 1939, the Dutch East Indies were supplying the US with over half of its needs for "no less than fifteen distinct commodities."

WWII radically changed the map of the Pacific, with the US emerging as the region's dominant power. US policymakers recognized that the region held great promise:

> These areas not only offer many markets for American products but are substantial producers of raw materials useful to our economy....Our merchant marine and commercial firms should be given the opportunity to take over a large portion of that trade formerly handled by the Japanese and their vessels.

George Kennan, Director of the Policy Planning Staff at the US State Department, noted that the US had "about 50% of the world's wealth but only 6.3 % of its population," and offered this advice:

> Our real task in the coming period is to devise a pattern of relationships which will permit us to maintain this position of disparity without positive detriment to our national security. We

should make a careful study to see what parts of
the Pacific and Far Eastern world are absolutely
vital to our security, and we should concentrate
our policy on seeing to it that those areas remain
in hands which we can control or rely on.

Indonesia, with its fertile soils, wealth of natural resources and strategic location, is certainly an
important area to "control or rely on." In a 1965
speech in Asia, Richard Nixon argued in favor of
bombing North Vietnam to protect the "immense
mineral potential" of Indonesia, which he later
referred to as "by far the greatest prize in the
southeast Asian area."

To protect its prizes, the US eventually killed
over four million people in Vietnam, Cambodia
and Laos between 1965 and 1975. In South
Vietnam alone, the war resulted in a million wid-
ows and 879,000 orphans. It destroyed 9000 out of
15,000 hamlets, almost 40,000 square miles of
farmland and 18,750 square miles of forest. Such
carnage indicates what the US would be willing to
support in Indonesia and East Timor.

In the late 1940s, US government and corporate leaders decided to support Indonesian independence over the continuing instability of Dutch
rule (as mentioned above). To their chagrin, however, the new Indonesian government became
highly nationalistic, anti-imperialist and non-
aligned. Worried that the area might move beyond
its control, Washington began (in the 1950s) to
curry favor with the Indonesian army, through military assistance and training programs.

The US soon reaped the benefits of this policy.
In 1965, using an alleged Communist plot to over-

throw the government as an excuse, pro-US General Suharto assumed control of the military and launched "one of the great slaughters of our time." Hundreds of thousands of Indonesians were killed, mostly landless peasants and members of the Communist Party of Indonesia (many of whose names had been supplied to the army by the US Embassy in Jakarta).

Suharto's government repealed the previous regime's "extremely restrictive" investment laws and paved the way for large-scale foreign investment. By the 1970s, the US was investing more in Indonesia than in any other Southeast Asian country, even the Philippines. Part of that trade was arms—the State Department estimates that US companies supplied about 90% of the weapons used during the invasion of East Timor.

The Suharto regime's support for US and Western political objectives, its liberal investment climate and its repressive labor conditions—the minimum wage is less than $2 a day—make it very attractive to Western companies. Under Suharto, Indonesia has developed into a major center for international business operations. Extensive mining, logging and oil extraction takes place there, as does manufacturing by a wide variety of US companies, including Nike and Levi Strauss.

Support for Indonesia's actions in East Timor and elsewhere is a small price to pay for the investment opportunities (and political support) Indonesia offers. So the US not only refused to condemn the invasion, but sharply increased aid to Indonesia since then.

In the year following the invasion, the Ford administration more than doubled its military assistance to Indonesia (to $146 million). In late 1977, when it looked as if Indonesia might run out of military equipment, the Carter "human rights" administration authorized $112 million in commercial arms sales to Jakarta, up almost 2000% from the previous fiscal year. US military sales peaked during the Reagan administration, exceeding $1 billion from 1982 to 1984. Over 2600 Indonesian military officers have received training in the US since the invasion of East Timor, under the International Military Education and Training Act (IMET).

As a State Department official explained shortly after the invasion: "The United States wants to keep its relations with Indonesia close and friendly. [It's] a nation we do a lot of business with."

Because the corporate media tend to follow the lead of their governments, people in the West learned almost nothing about Indonesia's brutal invasion and the ensuing war. When political parties in East Timor were working toward independence from Portugal (in 1975), a number of US newspapers reported on the process. But after the invasion, news of East Timor largely disappeared from the Western press.

The *Los Angeles Times* is a typical example. From August 1975 until the invasion on December 7, it ran sixteen articles dealing with East Timor. But from March 1976 to November 1979—during a time when Indonesia's occupation was described (in a report to the Australian parliament) as "indiscriminate killing on a scale unprecedented in post-World War II history"—East Timor wasn't mentioned once. (For more on the occupation, see pp. 50–65 below.) This neglect by the US media continued throughout the 1980s.

Australian support for Indonesia

It's important for Australia that the world under-stand that big countries cannot invade small neighbors and get away with it.

Australian Prime Minister Bob Hawke, 1990, referring to the Iraqi invasion of Kuwait

I don't see what you are getting excited about! The plain fact is that there are only 700,000 Timorese; what we are really concerned about is our relationship with 130,000,000 Indonesians.

An official of the Australian Foreign Affairs Department, circa the mid-1970s

Australia supported the first UN resolution con-demning the invasion, and both Prime Minister Fraser and his foreign minister publicly rejected Indonesia's absorption of East Timor. But this was largely due to massive popular opposition to the invasion. Beneath the surface, a different story was unfolding.

In January 1976, a month after the invasion, Australia's ambassador to Indonesia, Richard Woolcott, sent the following cable to Canberra:

On the Timor issue...we face one of those broad foreign-policy decisions which face most coun-tries at one timor [sic] or another. The Government is confronted by a choice between a moral stance, based on condemnation of Indonesia for the invasion of East Timor and on the assertion of the inalienable right of the people of East Timor to the right of self-determination, on the one hand, and a pragmatic and realistic acceptance of the longer-term inevitabilities of the situation on the other hand.

It is a choice between what might be described as Wilsonian idealism or Kissingerian realism. The former is more proper and principled but the longer-term national interest may well be served by the latter. We do not think we can have it both ways.

From the actions that followed, Australia's choice is clear. Prime Minister Fraser attempted to undermine support for FRETILIN within Australia. He seized a radio transmitter in Darwin that had been used to communicate with FRETILIN inside East Timor, and later denied Australian entry visas to FRETILIN leaders in exile. In addition, he reportedly gave an informal OK to Indonesia's takeover of East Timor during a visit with Suharto in Jakarta in October 1976.

Australian military assistance to Jakarta nearly doubled between 1975 and 1981. Australia now exchanges military intelligence with Indonesia and supplies both military hardware (like naval patrol boats) and training to ABRI.

US pressure may have had an influence on Australia's stance. It's been reported that high-ranking members of the Ford administration warned Fraser to back down from his criticisms of Indonesia's takeover of East Timor. Given US influence over Australia, it seems likely that

Australia would have complied. As a 1974 Australian Defense Department paper noted, "It is desirable...that Australian policy...pay regard to US interests and reactions, as an important ally and principal power in the Western strategic community."

Still, as with other Western powers, Australia's reasons for acquiescing to the invasion were largely economic. When Gough Whitlam became prime minister in 1972, he made it clear that Indonesia was the key to establishing stronger trade and investment connections with the Association of South East Asian Nations (ASEAN). Whitlam then stated, "It goes without saying that the number one [foreign policy] goal of my government is to strengthen relations with Indonesia."

Australia also has a major economic interest in Timor itself. Between Australia and East Timor lies the Timor Gap, which contains an underwater oil field that's thought to be one of the world's 25 richest deposits. As Ambassador Woolcott wrote in August 1975:

> We are all aware of the Australian defense interest in the Portuguese Timor situation but I wonder whether the Department has ascertained the interest of the Minister of the Department of Minerals and Energy in the Timor situation.... The present gap in the agreed sea border...could be much more readily negotiated with Indonesia...than with Portugal or an independent Portuguese Timor.
>
> I know I am recommending a pragmatic rather than a principled stand but that is what national interest and foreign policy is all about.

In January 1978, Australia became the only Western country ever to grant Indonesia official recognition of its sovereignty over East Timor; with that out of the way, the two countries entered into negotiations over the Timor Gap (a final agreement between them was signed in December 1989). A number of major oil companies—including Australian-based BHP, Dutch-based Shell and US-based Marathon—have already begun exploratory drilling there.

Portugal has filed a case against Australia with the International Court of Justice (which meets at the Hague, in the Netherlands), charging it with ignoring Portugal's legal status as the administering power of East Timor. A verdict against Australia (the decision is due in the summer of 1995) would force it to choose between losing enormous oil profits or abandoning the pretense of being a moral country.

Other supporters of Indonesia

Five months before the invasion, President Suharto visited Prime Minister Pierre Trudeau in Canada. One of the four items for discussion was "Prospects and Developments in Portuguese Timor." The meeting went well for Suharto—Canada pledged an additional CDN$200 million in aid. Several attempts to discover the nature of the discussions (by means of Access to Information requests) have been unsuccessful, but Canada's behavior following the invasion—under both Liberal and Conservative governments—provides some clues.

Canada abstained from voting on the first five UN General Assembly resolutions on East Timor, and voted *No* on the last three. Indonesia has consistently been among the top five recipients of Canada's direct, country-to-country aid, receiving CDN$40–$70 million annually.

Canadian investments in Indonesia are estimated at CDN$5 billion, with Inco Ltd.'s vast nickel-mining operation in Sulawesi leading the way. Drawn by cheap labor and lax environmental regulations, Inco has been expanding in Indonesia while laying off workers at home.

Canada has sold weapons to Indonesia—both directly and through sales to US arms companies who sell to Indonesia—and many of those weapons have been used in East Timor. Arms sales, halted in 1992, resumed under Prime Minister Jean Chrétien in 1993, whose government has identified Indonesia as a prime trade target. In the first year-and-a-half of Liberal government, Canada issued permits valued at CDN$5.7 million for arms exports to Indonesia. It's now Canada's largest export market in Southeast Asia, with two-way trade exceeding a billion dollars a year.

In November 1994, Chrétien signed a nuclear cooperation agreement with Indonesia, the first step toward providing it with Canadian nuclear reactor technology. This is alarming, since other countries have in the past used such technology to help develop nuclear weapons.

Japan cast negative votes on all eight UN General Assembly resolutions on East Timor. Its cozy relationship to the Suharto government can only be understood in light of the fact that, in 1975, it was the second largest foreign investor in Indonesia (now it's the largest).

According to a 1992 International Monetary Fund report, Japan received 37% of Indonesia's exports in 1991 (predominately oil and natural gas) and provided Indonesia with 25% of its imports. Japan is also the principal giver of economic aid to Jakarta, providing 69% of all the direct, country-to-country aid Indonesia received in 1992.

A Diplomatic White Paper from the Japanese government makes it quite clear how important Indonesia has become to Japan's future:

> Indonesia has a strong, mutually dependent relation with Japan through provision of oil and natural gas and acceptance of direct investment. And Indonesia is a very important country for Japan because it is located in an area with important international sea routes and because it has a large political influence in Southeast Asia.

East Timor—a tiny half-island with relatively few resources—can scarcely compete with what Indonesia has to offer.

In July 1975, when the Indonesians were in the early stages of Operation Komodo, the British ambassador to Indonesia wrote to the Foreign

Office that "the people of Portuguese Timor are in no condition to exercise their right to self-determination." But he added that it would be best not to acknowledge this openly:

> Certainly as seen from here it is in Britain's interest that Indonesia should absorb the territory as soon as and as unobtrusively as possible; and that if it come to the crunch and there is a row in the United Nations we should keep our heads down and avoid siding with the Indonesian government.

Britain abstained from all eight votes on East Timor in the UN General Assembly, and continues to sell arms to Indonesia. In 1978, the British government licensed the sale of eight British-made Hawk ground attack jets, which ABRI used in its saturation bombing during the encirclement and annihilation campaign (for more about this, see pp. 50–65 below). Recently, the sale of 24 more Hawk aircraft was approved. In 1992, Britain was the sixth largest foreign investor in Indonesia, and one source now ranks it as Jakarta's top arms supplier.

Billions of dollars in grants and bank credits have been bestowed on the genocidal Suharto regime by the Inter-Governmental Group on Indonesia (IGGI), a consortium of donor countries and organizations that includes Japan, the US, France, Britain, the Netherlands and Germany (the last two are also major arms suppliers to Indonesia). Since its inception in 1967, IGGI members have steadily increased their aid to Jakarta.

Today, Indonesia is the third largest debtor nation in the developing world (after Mexico and Brazil). Despite the Santa Cruz massacre, Western support for Indonesia continues unabated.

Indonesia's war of occupation

We are dying as a people and as a nation.

Carlos Belo, Bishop of Dili, 1989

In the first few months after the invasion began, ABRI forces could only capture major towns and villages and a few transportation corridors, despite heavy naval and aerial bombardment. In the rural areas, where the vast majority of the population lived, ABRI progressed at "a snail's pace" (in the words of the US Defense Intelligence Agency).

ABRI also suffered heavy casualties at the hands of FALINTIL (FRETILIN's army). Australian intelligence analysts estimated that there were more than 450 Indonesian military casualties in the first few weeks, and in the first four months of 1976, as many as 2000 Indonesian troops were killed.

This was largely because FRETILIN had expected the invasion for months. Well before December 1975, it had begun to establish bases and relocate its forces in the country's interior. With 2500 former full-time Portuguese troops, 7000 part-time militia, 10,000 reservists—plus civilians who had received military training following the civil war with the UDT—FALINTIL had a formidable contingent of fighters. In addition, it had a detailed knowledge of East Timor's geography and large supplies of weapons left by the Portuguese.

As a result, FRETILIN was able to maintain effective control over the majority of East Timorese territory for many months. Within the liberated areas, life continued as usual—schools and agricultural cooperatives continued to function, and FRETILIN radio continued to broadcast throughout the territory.

But beginning in September 1977, things took a turn for the worse. ABRI's plan was to push the resistance into the center of the country, where the fighters could be killed or captured, and to force the rural population to the coastal lowlands, where they could be more easily controlled. (Catholic sources called this "encirclement and annihilation.")

Using tens of thousands of ground troops and counterinsurgency aircraft called Broncos (newly acquired from the US, they were ideally suited for the rugged terrain of East Timor), ABRI forces began penetrating the interior of the island. Along the way, they bombed forested areas to defoliate ground cover and used chemical sprays to destroy crops and livestock.

Lourenco, a former UDT supporter who later began working with FRETILIN, described the annihilation of a section of FALINTIL's eastern zone:

> I was in Matebian [near Baguia], where it's all mountain and rocks....On 17 October 1978 some Indonesians got right to the bottom of

Matebian mountain and that's when we started to fight back. For those first two months, October and November, we were very successful and about 3000 Indonesians died. Then they got angry and scared to come close and started to bomb us from the air.

They bombed twice a day, in the morning and afternoon with four black planes. Their name I know now is Broncos, but we called them scorpions because they had a tail that curves up at the back like that insect. Their bombs left a big hole about two meters deep.

Then they got new supersonic planes. Our people were very frightened of those because you didn't even hear they were there until they were gone. Those supersonics would zoom along the valley so fast we couldn't shoot them....

We knew by radio from the south zone that the Indonesians had dropped four napalm bombs there. Then they dropped two of these on us. I saw all the flames and heard people shouting and screaming. I was on another mountain but I could see well....By foot it took half an hour to go down and up again, and by the time we got there everything was completely burnt.

We saw a whole area about fifty meters square all burnt, no grass, nothing except ash. On the rocks it was a brown reddish color and on the ground ash too, not ordinary grey ash, a sort of yellow ash, like beach sand. You couldn't see where bodies had been. There was nothing except ash and burnt rocks on the whole area, but we had heard those people screaming.

Additional Western military sales, including US F-5 jets and A-4 bombers and British Hawk ground attack aircraft, greatly increased ABRI's destructive capacity. With such attacks repeated over and over, FALINTIL had little chance of beating back the Indonesians, and many units had to surrender. Xavier, a guerrilla fighter, describes his capture by ABRI:

> In 1979 all our people, nearly 3000 from my Laclo area, were caught by the Indonesians near the main coast road where you pass to Manatutu and Baucau. We go to the highest point and stayed there for a month trying every way to get out.
>
> The Indonesians attacked us from the beach and from Manatutu, Dili and Baucau. All came together and surrounded us. Some fighters escaped and took guns back to other FALINTIL. I was captured because I was responsible, that was my position, I had to stay with my people, I couldn't leave. They captured me without my gun or I would be dead.
>
> We were interrogated, but we spoke no Bahasa Indonesia so a Timorese interpreted. He said, "Don't be afraid, always say something, say anything." The interpreter made up our answers. He was Timorese too, he tried to protect us. There were so many people to interrogate and we were all telling wrong things anyway. But when they took us to Dili, slowly they wiped out nearly all of us who'd been fighters. Spies and informers had time to do their work there.

By the time the encirclement and annihilation campaign ended in March 1979, "many thousands" of civilians and many top FRETILIN leaders were dead; others were captured or had surrendered. FALINTIL lost 80% of its troops and more than 90% of its weapons, and its internal and international lines of communication were completely severed. The captured troops, and the tens of thousands of civilians who fled from the mountains, were either relocated in "guarded camps" or deported to the offshore island of Atauro.

Its forces and weaponry devastated, FALINTIL was nonetheless able to regroup and reorganize—a pattern that was to be repeated several times in the next decade. Under the leadership of Xanana Gusmao, a local commander in the east, FALINTIL reorganized its forces into small, relatively independent units throughout the country.

The change in strategy and organization allowed it to mount more attacks on ABRI in 1980 than during the eighteen-month encirclement and annihilation campaign. Although FALINTIL couldn't reestablish control over any population centers, it was able to build a covert support network within Indonesian-controlled villages and to regain control of significant amounts of rural territory. ABRI casualties mounted and morale declined.

By March 1981 FRETILIN had established enough communication among its units to hold a national conference. There Xanana was elected head of FRETILIN and commander-in-chief.

In response to FRETILIN's resurgence, ABRI launched a new operation in mid-1981 that included something called a "fence of legs." About 80,000 East Timorese males, ranging in age from 8 to 50, were forced to walk in a line across the countryside in front of ABRI troops, protecting them from attack by FALINTIL guerrillas. The objective was to either flush out the guerrillas or to force them into the center of the island where they could be massacred. A participant, Cristiano da Costa, describes what it was like in one of many areas after the campaign:

> It started from all parts of East Timor, all driving towards Aitana, near Lakluta, that was to be the middle of the circle. The front line was Timorese forced to take part. When the circle was small enough, the army bombarded the area, then soldiers went to finish off any people left there.
>
> One week later I was forced to go up with a group of soldiers to do a final clean-up....We smelt the bodies before we found them. The heads had been cut off the first bodies, one woman and four men....The heads were on the other bodies I saw. We found three other men tied by the feet hanging upside down in trees...another two men were tied with their hands behind the trunks of trees. Their faces looked beaten and it looked like knife wounds to their stomachs.
>
> On the ground beside them there were six others, two women and two children and an old man and an old woman....There was dried blood on those bodies....The smell was very bad and the flies....It was not possible to identify those people; if they were my own brother or sister I could not know them.

Given only the most meager of provisions by the Indonesian military, many of the walkers in the "fence of legs" campaign starved to death. The operation also greatly disrupted agricultural production, leading to severe food shortages in most regions of the country.

While many FRETILIN groups surrendered or were slaughtered during the campaign, many evaded capture. By late 1982, FRETILIN had again reorganized and was launching a number of attacks all over the country (including one on Dili), putting local Indonesian military leaders increasingly on the defensive. A number of the officials decided to negotiate cease-fire agreements with FRETILIN, culminating in a country-wide cease-fire agreement on March 23, 1983. (ABRI and the Indonesian government hoped to keep the cease-fire secret and were greatly embarrassed when the news broke internationally.)

Within five months, however, ABRI Commander-in-Chief Benny Murdani unilaterally broke the cease-fire, declaring, "This time no fooling around. We are going to hit them without mercy." On August 17, 1983, Indonesia launched a new campaign.

But since FRETILIN had taken advantage of the cease-fire to consolidate its underground network in the resettlement villages, it could resist fiercely—even though it faced massive numbers of ABRI troops, as well as bombing from the air and sea. Once again, ABRI wasn't able to make any significant gains, and withdrew its troops to the major roads and population centers at the end of 1984.

During the latter half of the 1980s, ABRI launched a number of offensives, hoping to capture Xanana Gusmao, and it continued to use "fence of legs" operations. But, in large part, the military situation remains stalemated. ABRI's 15,000–20,000 troops control the main towns and other strategic locations, while FALINTIL's 1000–2000 guerrilla fighters roam the countryside. The resistance continues to have an extensive underground network in the towns as well.

You're Indonesians, damn it!

Indonesia's efforts to gain military control of East Timor have been the most violent and visible part of the occupation. But to achieve its long-term goal of "Indonesianizing" East Timor, it's used other, sometimes more insidious, forms of control against the civilian population.

Indonesianization is an ongoing process with a missionary and racist zeal. As a former Indonesian military commander described the task: "It is the new Indonesian civilization we are bringing. And it is not easy to civilize backward people."

The first step in this civilizing mission is physical control of the population. As early as April 1976, FRETILIN's underground radio network reported the existence of "guarded camps" in Indonesian-controlled areas. According to a July 1979 report by the Australian Council for Overseas Aid, there were fifteen camps with a population of 318,921 "displaced persons":

> [ABRI] ordered people to move from their own village or district into one or other of the fifteen centers as part of its strategy against FRETILIN. The strategy, which resembles counter-insurgency techniques employed against guerrillas in places such as Rhodesia,

Malaysia and Vietnam, has increased the Indonesian army's control over the local population and allowed it, in the words of an Indonesian parliamentarian, "to separate the people from the terrorists" (i.e., FRETILIN).

The forced relocation, combined with ABRI's brutal military campaign, disrupted local farming and resulted in widespread famine. In one camp, where 80% of its 8,000 inhabitants suffered from malnutrition, a visiting delegate from the International Committee of the Red Cross called the situation "as bad as Biafra and potentially as serious as Kampuchea." Forced labor, including carrying ammunition and supplies into combat areas, was also common.

The people in the camps were soon moved to "resettlement villages" that still exist today. They're located far away from the FALINTIL resistance, usually near asphalt roads to make them easily accessible to ABRI. When settling the camps, the occupation authorities deliberately broke up the traditional forms of social organization, placing people from the same villages, clans or hamlets in different resettlement villages, so that an organized resistance would be less likely to develop.

Within the villages, the military, police and *babinsas* (the eyes and ears of ABRI in the settlements) have kept a tight rein on the people. According to the former bishop of Dili, "The *babinsas* are everywhere. They are the ones who have to know about everything happening in the villages and the settlements. Everything has to be reported to them."

Justino, a visitor to the villages, describes the physical control and deplorable conditions found there:

> There were many resettlement villages—we call them concentration camps. There were fifty camps around Baucau in 1979. People were brought to a camp a long way from their own place. They missed their land and their belongings, their ancestors and *lulik* [sacred] things. The camps were for the Indonesian military to control people and keep them away from Resistance fighters....
>
> The camps were open areas, no fences, with small Timorese houses made of bamboo that last a few months—people built them themselves. To get into a camp you had to get special permission. I visited sometimes with a priest.
>
> I didn't talk much to [the people in the camps] because there were informers and the military were always there, but I saw a lot of sick and starving people and I know many died because they weren't allowed to move far, they couldn't farm or collect enough food. If they went far outside the camp, they were suspected of contacting guerrillas and could be shot or put in prison or disappear.

A second step in Indonesianization is control of the economy. Soon after the invasion, Indonesian interests simply took over former Portuguese colonial enterprises. Indonesian authorities also began to take lands traditionally held by groups of hamlets (maintaining that no one owns traditionally-held lands, since there aren't any formal tenants) and to give them to local officials or pro-Indonesian native rulers.

Then, beginning in 1991, the Indonesian authorities requested that all private property owners convert their property certificates from the Portuguese to the Indonesian system. Since there's been massive dislocation from the war, and since Indonesia requires that land be "owner-occupied," this new system threatens both private landholdings by East Timorese living in exile abroad and traditionally-held lands, and will further concentrate land in the hands of Indonesian interests.

But even those who still work their land face economic control. Farmers who grow coffee, for example, are forced to sell it to P. T. Denok, a military monopoly set up by General Benny Murdani and a few associates immediately after the invasion. As an Indonesian military commander in East Timor remarked, it was "the only company that landed with the marines. They came together."

P. T. Denok's monopoly has resulted in declining incomes for small East Timorese farmers, while the company's coffee profits have allowed it to diversify. One of its subsidiaries, P. T. Scent, has a monopoly on the collection and sale of sandalwood, which have increased significantly under the Indonesian occupation.

Today the P. T. Batara Indra Group controls P. T. Denok, P. T. Scent and ten other subsidiaries in East Timor. The group owns Dili's only movie theater and its three luxury hotels, controls the territory's marble production and imports a wide variety of consumer products. According to a leading Indonesian academic, the group virtually controls the East Timorese economy. Although the companies are nominally owned by civilians, there's little doubt that ABRI, or interests close to the military, ultimately control them.

Outside the military-controlled areas of the economy, Indonesian business interests almost completely dominate East Timorese commerce. Indonesian entrepreneurs have filled the economic vacuum created by the slaughter and flight of most East Timor's ethnic Chinese. Basic industries that produced agricultural tools, clothing, household goods and building materials during the Portuguese era have largely disappeared, and these goods are now imported from Indonesia. A 1980 Indonesian anthropological study warned:

> There needs to be some form of protection given to prevent big business commoditizing land and commercializing everyday life in the more remote areas. Without protection the East Timorese will simply become victims of moneyed interests from other regions [of Indonesia].

A 1990 follow-up study stated that the fear that the East Timorese subsistence economy will be "marginalized by capitalists and 'foreign' [i.e. Indonesian] entrepreneurs is well founded."

A third step of Indonesianization is control of the educational system, which completely neglects any information about East Timor that doesn't correspond to Jakarta's official viewpoint. Indonesian [Bahasa Indonesia] is the only language allowed in schools. Military culture is also taught, and all students must memorize *Pancasila*, the supposed ideological basis of Indonesian society.

The school system also strongly encourages physical education (which is closely connected to the militarization of society) and membership in *Pramuka,* the state-controlled scout organization. Said one refugee, "There is a lot of physical education, less academic work and considerable singing of songs—the Indonesian anthem, the *Pancasila* set to music which you must memorize, school songs and songs patriotic to Indonesia."

But while Indonesia asserts that the number of schools in East Timor has increased dramatically since the invasion, illiteracy remains high (in 1989, it was estimated at 92%). This is probably due as much to East Timorese resistance to Indonesianization as it is to Jakarta's misplaced educational priorities.

Not trusting that all these tactics will sufficiently Indonesianize the local population, Jakarta has resorted to other, more severe measures. They've begun a World Bank-funded program to decrease the birth rate of East Timorese women. A 1986 letter from inside East Timor describes the coercive nature of this program:

> Officials of the state planning program are present in every little village and hamlet to make people limit their number of children, and each family is only allowed to have three children. In the interior the military force our women to receive injections, and pills are being distributed to them for the same effect. All the women are being forced to take part in this. It is one way the enemy has to make our ethnic identity disappear.

International human rights groups and many East Timorese have accused Jakarta's family planning program of sterilizing East Timorese women without their knowledge, especially in the aftermath of the encirclement and annihilation campaign. Whether this is true or not, Jakarta's motives in attempting to lower the birth rate are certainly highly suspect. As the bishop of Dili, Carlos Belo, points out, "With so many dead, we have no population problem here."

While attempting to limit the East Timorese population, Indonesian authorities actively encourage Indonesians from throughout the country to migrate to East Timor. Under the guise of relieving population pressures in the relatively crowded islands like Java and Bali, and filling "empty" land in places like East Timor, Jakarta uses this "transmigration" program to try to create a pan-Indonesian identity and to serve the security needs of the military.

Land given to the transmigrants was either formerly owned by East Timorese who were forcibly relocated, or is deemed "underutilized" by the Indonesian authorities. In neither situation are the former owners compensated.

Jakarta hopes that transmigration will help East Timor's population reach one million by the year 2000, although the actual number who have transmigrated so far is not very high. One 1989 estimate stated that only about 500 families from outside East Timor have settled in the territory, mostly in areas that border West Timor. Recent reports indicate that the transmigration has continued; there was a target of 425 families for 1992–93.

Another kind of migration—"spontaneous" or "voluntary" migration of people from all over Indonesia—poses an even more serious threat to East Timorese ethnic identity. Thousands of

Indonesians have migrated to East Timor in search of land, economic opportunities or government jobs.

One report states that 25,000 heads of families from other islands of Indonesia voluntarily migrated to East Timor during 1989 alone. In 1992, an estimated 100,000 Indonesians were living in East Timor (out of a total population about 750,000).

Another thrust of Indonesianization is Jakarta's attempt to make its invasion of East Timor look like a civil war between East Timorese in favor of integration with Indonesia and those opposed to it. Two ABRI battalions of East Timorese have been formed, mostly made up of conscripts. ABRI has also formed local militias, often with compulsory participation.

"Jorge," now a refugee in Australia, describes his experience in one such militia:

> I was in high school, a student, when the war started in Timor. I had no political ties, didn't belong to any party. My friends and I were forced to join the Indonesian army. We were warned; all who didn't join the army had to take the consequences. That means that they say you are communist. None of us wanted to but there was no way not to fight. If you don't fight, you get killed yourself.
>
> I went on operations to kill other Timorese, ordinary people. Then I felt strange. None of us felt good. At first we are sad, we have remorse, but after two or three years, it was easy. You get used to killing....
>
> I was forced to kill my best friend. I don't want to talk about it. I don't feel good when I

think about it....They knew he was my friend and I was forced to shoot him. They do these things to test you.

Recent developments

The concept of realpolitik [is] the denial of the individual conscience, the death of the conscience of a people.

Xanana Gusmao, Defense Plea, May 17, 1993

In response to international pressure generated by the Santa Cruz massacre, Indonesia has continuously claimed that it is reducing the number of its troops in East Timor, and that most of the remaining troops are engaged in development projects, like the construction of houses, roads and bridges, and not in combat. Many observers, including Bishop Belo of Dili, dismiss such claims, but even if they were true, ABRI could still easily respond to any military threats that might arise by simply dispatching two battalions of combat-ready troops it has stationed in Java.

In any case, as the ABRI commander in East Timor stated a couple of years ago, "the main security threat is not...small, roaming guerrilla units but the expanding anticolonial movement among young East Timorese." In an attempt to wipe out the underground resistance, ABRI has stepped up the search for "two-faced" East Timorese who pretend to be pro-Indonesian publicly but are really East Timorese nationalists.

This strategy paid off. In November 1992, ABRI captured Xanana Gusmao, the commander-in-chief of FALINTIL, in a Dili safe house that was the home of an East Timorese police officer. In May 1993, an Indonesian court in Dili sentenced Xanana to life imprisonment, which President Suharto has since commuted to 20 years.

In spite of the repression, the resistance lives on—as the world was reminded in November 1994, when 29 East Timorese students and workers jumped out of taxis coming from different directions and scaled the spiked fence of the US embassy in Jakarta. Camped out in the embassy parking lot, the demonstrators called upon Bill Clinton—who was there for a trade conference—to voice support for East Timorese self-determination and for the withdrawal of Indonesian troops from their country. (He didn't, and after twelve days, the demonstrators left for exile in Portugal.)

The day after the embassy sit-in began, a pro-independence rally took place after a mass in Dili commemorating the victims of the Santa Cruz massacre. With dozens of foreign journalists present, scores of courageous young people, marching with FRETILIN banners, called for independence and Clinton's support. Following the peaceful march, over a thousand East Timorese youths rioted in Dili, attacking Indonesian-owned homes, stores and hotels, burning cars and clashing with police.

Frequent violent protests continued for at least two weeks. Several protestors were reported dead and hundreds were arrested. As the head of the East Timorese Catholic Church, Bishop Carlos Belo, recently stated, "the situation is as bad as ever....We live in a scorched land."

(As the only East Timorese institution that has survived the Indonesian invasion and occupation, the Church serves as a psychological and spiritual refuge for the vast majority of the East Timorese, over 90% of whom are Catholic. Under the leadership of Bishop Belo, who was recently nominated for the Nobel Peace Prize, the Church has become one of the most outspoken defenders of human rights in East Timor, incurring the ire and deep suspicion of the Indonesian authorities.)

A new, more broadly based, umbrella organization now represents all the groups within East Timor that are dedicated to national self-determination, including FRETILIN and the UDT. Called the CNRM, or National Council of Maubere Resistance, it was formed by Xanana Gusmao and others in 1989. *(Maubere* was a contemptuous term the Portuguese used when referring to the East Timorese. In the 1970s, FRETILIN transformed it into a term of pride.)

FALINTIL, originally FRETILIN's army, has become the nonpartisan military wing of CNRM— that is, of the entire resistance. It currently numbers about 600–800 full-time guerrilla fighters and approximately 1500 reserves. According to its new commander-in-chief, Konis Santana, FALINTIL would grow quickly if it had enough weaponry.

In addition to Santana, the CNRM today has two other leaders. International diplomatic activity is handled by José Ramos-Horta, and Laran

Sabalae is in charge of organizing clandestine networks within towns and disseminating information to the outside world. (Although imprisoned, Xanana Gusmao remains the CNRM's supreme commander.)

In 1992, the CNRM presented a comprehensive peace proposal to the European Parliament in Brussels, and later to the UN. It proposes a three-phase process that would take at least five years and would culminate in an East Timorese referendum on self-determination. Indonesia has ignored the proposal, but it serves as a basis for CNRM diplomatic activity and is becoming increasingly known throughout the world.

Recently, the CNRM joined forces with FRETILIN and the UDT to form the Coordinating Committee of the Diplomatic Front (CCFD), which will provide "unified diplomatic representation" for the East Timorese nationalist movement.

East Timor's future

The will of the people shall be the basis of the authority of the government.

Article 21 (3) of the *Universal Declaration of Human Rights,* adopted by the UN General Assembly, December 10, 1948

What are the prospects for East Timorese self-determination? Some people hoped that a more liberal political climate would develop within Indonesia, but those hopes were dashed by the 1993 "re-election" of Suharto as the country's president and of General Try Sutrisno, the commander of ABRI at the time of the Santa Cruz massacre, as vice-president.

Nevertheless, a number of Indonesian leaders understand the high price Jakarta is paying for its occupation of East Timor. (As Indonesia's foreign minister put it in March 1992, "Timor is like a sharp piece of gravel in our shoes.") Although some military brass and big business owners have gotten rich off of East Timor, it's never become the prosperous province that Indonesia hoped it would, and probably 20,000 Indonesian soldiers— or even more—have lost their lives in the war.

East Timor has been a disaster for Jakarta diplomatically as well. A number of Western European countries, as well as the European Parliament, have increased diplomatic activity on the issue of East Timor. UN-sponsored talks between Indonesia and Portugal resumed in 1992, and this time they're accompanied by consultations with East Timorese who are independent of Jakarta.

Recently, Indonesia's foreign minister ended Jakarta's long-standing refusal to meet with pro-independence East Timorese and sat down with the CNRM's José Ramos-Horta. Still, Indonesia refuses to discuss self-determination for East Timor, and maintains a heavy military presence there.

In September 1992, in response to a groundswell of grassroots pressure following the Santa Cruz massacre, the US Congress cut off IMET (International Military Education and Training) funds worth $2.3 million to Indonesia. This was the first time Washington had reduced aid to Indonesia since the invasion of East Timor—and it occurred in spite of strong opposition from the Bush administration and major US corporations.

The end of the Cold War and the election of Bill Clinton—who called US policy toward East Timor "unconscionable" during his campaign—also seemed to be hopeful signs. Indeed, in August 1993, Clinton's State Department refused to approve the Jordanian government's proposed sale of four US-made F-5E fighter jets to Indonesia. And in early 1994, public pressure forced the State Department to ban the sale of small arms to Indonesia.

At the March 1993 meeting of the UN Human Rights Commission in Geneva, the US reversed its previously intransigent stance and cosponsored a resolution condemning Indonesian human rights violations in East Timor. A number of Western countries followed suit—including Australia, which would have otherwise voted against the resolution—indicating the key role the US could play in determining East Timor's future.

Nevertheless, the Clinton administration continues to provide significant economic assistance to Indonesia—$180 million worth over the last two years through the Consultative Group on Indonesia, a consortium of donor countries and organizations. The CGI was set up following the Santa Cruz massacre, when there was increased pressure to link aid to Indonesia to human rights. To prevent this from happening, Jakarta disbanded the Netherlands-chaired IGGI (see p. 49 above) in early 1992 and replaced it with the CGI, chaired by the World Bank. CGI members pledged about $5 billion to Indonesia in each of the last three years (1992, 1993 and 1994).

The US also sold $30 million in weaponry to Indonesia in direct, government-to-government transactions in 1993 alone. Arms sales by US corporations—which require State Department approval—are estimated at $57 million for 1994. The Clinton administration is trying to reinstate Indonesia's IMET funding—and has sidestepped the ban in any case by letting Indonesia purchase the training. Joint US-Indonesia military exercises continue.

Nonetheless, the small but significant changes that have occurred in US policy demonstrate the effectiveness that grassroots pressure can have. Since the Santa Cruz massacre, East Timor has become an issue of considerable debate, and both members of Congress and the public are increasingly challenging the US government's complicity in Indonesia's genocidal policies.

In the US and Canada, East Timor solidarity groups (both called ETAN) have played a crucial role in publicizing their governments' complicity in the Indonesian occupation. These organizations now have active chapters in several cities. For information on how to contact them, see *What you can do* on p. 77.

There are also East Timor solidarity groups in Australia, Belgium, Brazil, Britain, Fiji, Finland, France, Germany, Ireland, Italy, Japan, Malaysia, Mozambique, the Netherlands, New Zealand, Norway, the Philippines, Portugal, South Korea, Thailand, Sri Lanka, Sweden and other countries. Even within Indonesia itself, significant parts of the pro-democracy and human rights movements are now in favor of East Timorese self-determination, a position unthinkable prior to the Santa Cruz massacre.

As their resistance has demonstrated so dramatically through the years, the will of the East Timorese people for independence will be difficult to eradicate. Xanana Gusmao once said, "To resist is to win." Through its resistance to Indonesian tyranny, East Timor survives.

Those of us outside of East Timor can help the the long-suffering East Timorese not only to survive but to live. Strong public pressure on the US and other Western countries can force Indonesia to withdraw, and can bring about an internationally supervised vote on self-determination.

My visit to East Timor

East Timor has been open to foreign tourists since 1989, but few researchers or journalists have been allowed in since the Santa Cruz massacre. So when I went there in July 1992, I called myself a tourist.

My flight from West Timor to Dili gave me my first glimpse of the half-island I'd been studying for the last few years. Dominated by mountains, East Timor's terrain is often quite rugged, but it's also quite beautiful.

As my flight approached Dili's Comoro Airport, the rural landscape gave way to a medium-sized, Mediterranean-looking town, nestled around one of Timor's few natural harbors. With a population of about 100,000, Dili is East Timor's largest city. Since it suffered extensive bombing in World War II, many of its buildings are fairly new, but much of its architecture still bears the stamp of its Portuguese colonial past.

The first day, I tried to get my bearings. Walking around Dili, I could get a sense of the diverse ethnic origins of the East Timorese. The population is largely a mixture of Malay, Makassarese and Papuan peoples who speak a number of indigenous languages. Tetum serves as the indigenous *lingua franca* and is spoken and understood in most parts of the country. Indonesian and—to a far lesser extent—Portuguese are also spoken. My very limited Portuguese and Indonesian (combined with English, Spanish and French) allowed me to communicate with many of the people whom I encountered.

It didn't take long to get a sense of the resentment and fear that permeate East Timorese life. In Indonesia itself, the streets are full of bustling activity, and a foreigner hears the ubiquitous greeting of "Hello, Mister" from young faces. In Dili, the streets are more deserted, and when you pass people, many seem afraid even to say hello.

On my first day, I stopped a young man on the street for directions to the nearest restaurant, and asked him how things were in Dili. His vague, hushed reply—that there were many problems—warned me not to press further.

His fear wasn't hard to understand. There are dozens of military installations throughout the city, and truckloads of young Indonesian soldiers frequently drive through the streets. Less obvious but even more pernicious is the extensive network of spies, and paid or coerced informants (often East Timorese), that permeates the city.

A Catholic priest in Dili told me he feared spies in his own congregation. In central East Timor, a seminarian described the situation as "a prison" in which "we are slaves of the Indonesians." In the town of Baucau, a young man darted out of the bushes near my hotel and thrust into my hand a letter for the International Committee of the Red Cross. (He probably thought I was with the Red Cross, since it's the only international organization with a presence in the country.) He disappeared before I could talk with him.

In Los Palos, a town in the eastern end of the island, a teenager told me of seven friends accused of associating with the underground resistance. They had been arrested and severely beaten until their faces were "black."

Also in the eastern end of the island, a nun whom I'll call Sister Maria told me the story of Rosa, a young girl enrolled in a local Catholic school. The nuns were having great difficulty getting Rosa to accept the Christian concept of forgiveness. But then she told them why she couldn't forgive her enemy.

A few years ago, some ABRI soldiers came to Rosa's home and took away her older brother, who they accused of ties to the resistance. Too afraid even to inquire about his whereabouts, the family had no idea where the army had taken him, or if he was even alive. A month later, the soldiers returned to Rosa's home with a bag. Inside it was her brother's head.

Understandably, stories like these frightened me—and with good reason. On a number of occasions, I was followed, and there were times when a "friend" would ask far too many questions of me.

The photographer who had met my flight and snapped pictures of deplaning passengers subsequently appeared at a number of restaurants where I was eating.

I later learned that he met all planes or ferries from West Timor and other islands. Twice he came to my hotel, pretending to socialize with the proprietors. After a couple of weeks, it became even more obvious that I was attracting attention from Indonesian intelligence. When I visited a town about 25 miles from Dili, an East Timorese who worked for the Indonesians came looking for me only a half hour after I arrived, and told me that the military commander of the district wanted to talk to me.

When we met, the commander (who had studied English at Fort Benning, Georgia) told me he simply wanted to "welcome me" to town. We were then joined by the chief of police, a man in his fifties who proudly flexed his biceps to show his youthful vigor. Then they asked me a number of questions: *What did I know about Santa Cruz? Why, among all the great places in Indonesia, did I choose to come to East Timor? How did the "reality" of East Timor compare with the picture presented to the outside world?* I did my best to sound like an ignorant American tourist.

I doubt I fooled anyone, since the Indonesians' interest in me continued. Two days later, someone stood outside the window of my low-budget hotel for a couple of hours, peering through a little hole in the window as I lay in bed.

Although such experiences left me almost constantly fearful, my anxiety paled in comparison to the constant fear that permeates everyday life in

East Timor. It would be difficult to find an East Timorese who has not lost a family member or a close friend to the Indonesian military.

Yet to report on the terror and tragedy alone would be only part of the story. In most places I visited, there was also evidence of the resilient, defiant spirit that's fueled almost two decades of guerrilla war and a national resistance movement. A small but vibrant guerrilla army and an extensive underground are also active in towns and villages throughout the country.

Through a combination of my own luck and the eagerness of the East Timorese resistance to communicate with foreigners, I made contact with members of the resistance. A few times I was led or driven at night to places where information, documents and rolls of film were passed to me to carry to the outside world.

But usually the signs of resistance were more subtle. People would flash me the *V* sign for victory or approach me to ask that I tell the United Nations to help, and that I ask the US government to stop sending military and economic aid to Indonesia.

Everywhere I went it was obvious that Indonesia had failed to win the hearts and minds of the vast majority of the East Timorese. As a prominent figure associated with the resistance said to me several days before my departure, "Politically we have won. However, it is a question of force—something we do not have."

It was clear to most East Timorese with whom I spoke that—barring radical changes in Jakarta—their fate lies in cities like Canberra, Tokyo, London, and, most importantly, Washington, where decisions to support Suharto's regime and supply it with arms have provided Indonesia with the means to carry out its genocidal policies.

I left Timor unharmed, probably because the authorities were never quite sure who I was and what I was doing there, but also because my American identity afforded me some protection. Needless to say, the East Timorese have no such protection—as the death, often by torture, of more than 200,000 of them demonstrates.

What you can do

In this brutal world, there are many causes worth putting your time, effort and money into. But there's probably nothing you can do that will save more lives, per dollar or hour you invest, than to support an East Timor solidarity group. Here's how to get in touch with them:

- East Timor Action Network (ETAN/US), PO Box 1182, White Plains NY 10602; phone: 914 428 7299; fax: 914 428 7383; e-mail: cscheiner@igc.apc.org. (This is also the UN Office for the International Federation for East Timor.)

- East Timor Alert Network (ETAN/Canada), PO Box 562, Station P, Toronto M5S 2T1; phone & fax: 416 531 5850; e-mail: etantor@web.apc.org.

- For information on solidarity groups in other countries, contact either of the above organizations or the East Timorese resistance itself (CNRM, PO Box 2155, Darwin NT 0801, Australia; phone: 61 69 855 678; fax: 61 69 855 622).

Arthur Naiman

Recommended reading

*So our stories have made you sad, you tell me.
Yes, this I can understand...but tears are not the
right response. For every painful story there is
one of beauty, one to learn from....You must
never forget the art of enjoyment. Otherwise
the pain of survival will crush you.*

> Gaspar, a guerrilla with the Guatemalan
> National Revolutionary Union

Dunn, James. *Timor: A People Betrayed.* The
    Jacaranda Press, Queensland, Australia. 1983.
    Out-of-print; check the library.

McMillan, Andrew. *Death in Dili.* Hodder &
    Stoughton, Rydalmere NSW Australia. 1992.
    *Available from The Australia East Timor
    Association (AETA), PO Box 93, Fitzroy,
    Victoria 3065 Australia.*

The TAPOL Bulletin (a bimonthly update on politi-
    cal and human rights throughout Indonesia).
    The Indonesian Human Rights Campaign,
    111 Northwood Road, Thornton Heath, Surrey,
    CR7 8HW, United Kingdom; phone: 81 771
    2904, fax: 81 653 0322.

Taylor, John G. *Indonesia's Forgotten War:
    The Hidden History of East Timor.* Zed Books,
    London. 1991. *Available from ETAN/US (see
    p. 77 for contact information).*

Turner, Michele. *Telling: East Timor Personal
    Testimonies 1942–1992.* New South Wales
    University Press, PO Box 1, Kensington NSW
    Australia. 1992. *Available from AETA
    (see McMillan above).*

Notes

Sources for the facts in this book are listed below by page numbers and brief subject descriptions *(in italics)*. Full publication data is given the first time a work is cited. If a work is mentioned in the *Recommended Reading* section on the facing page, it's **boldfaced** when it's first cited below; this tells you to look in that section for the publication information.

Preface

6 • *1965 massacre.* The CIA estimates the number killed at a quarter million and Indonesian state security at half a million, but Amnesty International, a much more reliable source—and one with no ax to grind—estimates "many more than one million" victims. For more on this, see Noam Chomsky, *Z Magazine,* 9/90, 15–23, and Benedict Anderson and Ruth McVey, "What Happened in Indonesia?," letter to the editor in *The New York Review,* 6/1/78, 40–42.

7 • *200,000+ dead.* Asia Watch, *Human Rights in Indonesia and East Timor,* Human Rights Watch (New York), 1989, 253.

Introduction

8 • *Anderson quote.* Tom Hyland, AAP Bureau Chief in Melbourne, article reprinted in the *Newsletter of the East Timor Talks Campaign,* Fitzroy, Australia, 9/92, reporting a talk by Anderson in Melbourne. He expressed similar views at a talk at Harvard at about the same time.

8–9 • *Western attitudes.* Geoffrey Gunn, *A Critical View of Western Scholarship and Journalism,* Manila, 1994. Most of the material has been available since the late 1970's. See Noam Chomsky and Edward S. Herman, *The Washington Connection and Third World Fascism: The Political Economy of Human Rights, Vol. 1,* South End Press (Boston),1979, and much subsequent work.

8–9 • *Woolcott cables.* Noam Chomsky, *Towards a New Cold War,* Pantheon,1982.

11 • *Great souls care little....* Aaron Burr quoted "in the manner of" Napoleon, in Henry Adams, *History of the United States of America during the Administration of Thomas Jefferson,* Library of America, 1986, 132.

13 • *Timor's petroleum smells better....* John Pilger, "Blood on the Hands of the Mates," *Green Left,* 4/20/94.

13 • *Boston Globe headline.* Story by Brian McGrory, 11/12/92.

14 • *Lloyd George quote.* See Noam Chomsky, *Year 501: The Conquest Continues,* South End, 1993, Ch. 1.

The Santa Cruz Massacre

16 • *Eyewitness report.* Allan Nairn, *The New Yorker,* 12/9/91, 41.

16 • *Hundreds killed at Santa Cruz.* National Council of Maubere Resistance (CNRM) press release, East Timor, 9/3/92.

16 • *Cold-blooded massacre.* Max Stahl, "Massacre Among the Graves," *Independent on Sunday* (London), 11/17/91.

16 • *Soldiers later kill wounded.* Max Stahl, "Dili, the bloody Aftermath," *Sydney Morning Herald,* 2/12/94.

17 • *International and Indonesian reaction to Santa Cruz.* Matthew Jardine, "Forgotten Genocide: A little attention, at last, for East Timor," *The Progressive,* 12/92, 19–20.

Portuguese rule

18 • *East Timor sits still.* José Ramos-Horta, *Funu: the Unfinished Saga of East Timor,* Red Sea Press (Trenton, NJ), 1987, 14.

18 • *Portuguese arrive in Timor.* Jill Jolliffe, *East Timor: Nationalism and Colonialism,* University of Queensland Press, 1978, 22–23; **Taylor**, 2–3.

18 • *Early Portuguese trade.* Jolliffe, 22–23; Taylor, 2–3, 8.

18 • *Arrival of* Topasses. **Dunn**, 16–17; C. R. Boxer, "Portuguese Timor: A Rough Island Story: 1515–1960," *History Today,* May 1960, 350.

19 • *Power struggles for control.* William Burton Sowash, "Colonial Rivalries in Timor," *The Far Eastern Quarterly,* 5/48, 230; Taylor, 4.

19 • *Official division of the island.* Taylor, 12.

19 • *Wallace describes Timor.* Alfred Russel Wallace, *The Malay Archipelago: The Land of the Orang-utan, and the Bird of Paradise,* MacMillan, vol. 1, 1869, 307.

19 • *Portugal shows new interest in East Timor.* Jolliffe, 34; Taylor, 10.

19 • *Cash crops and forced labor.* Gerard J. Telkamp, "The Economic Structure of an Outpost in the Outer Islands in the Indonesian Archipelago: Portuguese Timor 1850–1975," in P. Creutzberg, *Between Peoples and Statistics: Essays on Modern Indonesian History,* Martin Nijhoff, 1979, 78; G. Clarence-Smith, "Planters and Small Holders in Portuguese Timor in the 19th and 20th Centuries," *Indonesia Circle,* Mar 92, 15–30.

20 • *1910–12 revolt.* Jolliffe, 36–39; Dunn, 19–20.

20 • *Rise of Timorese elite.* Taylor, 16; Dunn, 7–8.

20 • *Catholic schools.* A. Diaz de Rábago, "Portuguese Timor," *New Catholic Encyclopedia,* Vol. 14, McGraw Hill, 1967, 166.

20 • *Dili economically backward.* Dunn, 21.

World War II and after

21 • *Japanese invasion and occupation.* Dunn, 25–26; **Turner**, 3.

21 • *Shouachi's memories.* Quoted in Turner, 52.

22 • *Japan might have ignored Timor.* Dunn, 23–26; Turner, 4; Taylor, 14.

22 • *Portuguese Timor rebuilt.* Taylor, 14.

22 • *Serious revolt.* Taylor, 21; Jolliffe, 48–49; Dunn, 33–34

22 • *Church encourages patriotism.* Dunn, 51.

23 • *US assists Indonesian independence.* Malcolm Caldwell, "Oil and Imperialism in East Asia," *Journal of Contemporary Asia,* No. 3, 1971, 22.

23 • *Mass media in Portuguese Timor.* Telkamp, 77; Dunn, 39.

23 • *Jesuit education.* Dunn, 53; Taylor, 27.

24 • *Dissidents meet clandestinely.* Jolliffe, 55–56.

The struggle for independence

24 • *Murdani quote.* Speech translated and distributed by **TAPOL**.

25 • *MFA's attitude to colonies.* Taylor, 25.

25 • *Three options for Timor.* Dunn, 59.

25 • *No Portuguese action on options.* Helen Hill, *FRETILIN: The Origins, Ideologies and Strategies of a Nationalist Movement in East Timor,* M.A. Thesis, Monash University, Australia, 1978, 113.

25 • *UDT formed.* Taylor, 26; Ramos-Horta, 29–31; Dunn, 61.

25–26 • *ASDT formed.* Dunn, 63; Ramos-Horta, 35; Taylor, 27.

26 • *UDT and ASDT leaders.* Jolliffe, 69; Taylor 27; Dunn, 64.

26 • *APODETI and Indonesian intelligence.* Taylor, 23, 27–28; Dunn, 71.

26–27 • *UDT loses ground to the ASDT.* Dunn, 62.

27 • *Malik reassures Ramos-Horta.* Ramos-Horta, 41–43; Dunn, 65–66; Taylor, 29. For a copy of Malik's letter, see Jolliffe, 66.

27 • *Australia fails to support independence.* Dunn, 67; Ramos-Horta, 75–77; Taylor 29–30.

27 • *FRETILIN'S program.* Taylor, 42; Ramos-Horta, 37.

27 • *FRETILIN most popular party.* Dunn, 69; Taylor, 35; Jolliffe, 89–90.

27 • *Lisbon calls independence unrealistic.* Dunn, 84–85; Taylor, 36–37.

27–28 • *Coalition formed and APODETI rejects MFA offer.* [Helen] Hill, 115–16; Taylor, 38–39.

28 • *Outcome of first decolonization talk.* Taylor, 39; Jolliffe, 113.

28 • *Operation Komodo.* Dunn, 116; Taylor, 31.

28 • *Gough Whitlam quote. Sinar Harapan* (Jakarta), 9/74, quoted in Taylor, 32.

28 • *Whitlam's comments favorable to Indonesia.* Dunn, 110–11, Taylor, 32.

28 • *Komodo intensified.* Taylor, 39–40.

29 • *Komodo succeeds in breaking up coalition.* Jolliffe, 115–16; Taylor, 41–43, 46.

29 • *UDT coup.* Taylor, 50–51; Jolliffe, 115–19.

29 • *UDT driven into West Timor.* Carmel Budiardjo & Liem Soei Liong, *The War Against East Timor,* Zed Books, 1984, 55; Taylor, 51; Dunn, 180; Jolliffe, chapter 4.

29 • *Refugees forced to support* integration. Jolliffe, 145.

29 • *UDT leader not wanting to sign petition.* Dunn, 181–82.

30 • *People support* de facto *government.* Dunn, 210.

30 • *Lisbon postpones peace talks.* Ramos-Horta, 59.

30 • *CIA confirms Indonesian aggression.* Dale Van Atta and Brian Toohey. "The Timor Papers" (Parts I & II), *The National Times* (Australia), 5/30–6/5; 6/6–12, 1982.

30 • *ABRI attacks East Timorese towns.* Budiardjo & Liem, 20–21.

31 • *Recognition comes slowly.* Jolliffe, 216–17.

Indonesia invades

31 • *FRETILIN broadcast.* Quoted in Budiardjo & Liem, 1984, 15

31 • *Malik minimalizes East Timorese losses.* AAP-Reuter dispatch from Jakarta, *Canberra Times,* 4/1/77, quoted in Chomsky & Herman, 176.

31–32 • *Catholic bishop reports killing everywhere. TAPOL Bulletin,* Sep 83.

32 • *Eloise's report.* Turner, 107.

32–33 • *Mr. Siong's report.* Turner. 104–5.

33 • *ABRI looting.* Taylor, 69–70; Dunn, 285.

33 • Olinda's report. Turner, 146–47.

33–34 • ABRI rape and abuse East Timorese women. Dunn, 285–86.

34 • Edhina's report. Turner, 109–10.

34 • Anti-Chinese sentiment. Taylor, 69; **McMillan**, 67.

35 • Invasion expands and number of East Timorese killed. Budiardjo & Liem, 1984, 15, 23; Taylor, 71; Dunn, 292–93, 302–303.

35 • Indonesia-staged event. Dunn, 298; Taylor, 73–74.

35 • Eyewitness account of People's Assembly. Hamish McDonald, "Staging the Rites of Integration," *Far Eastern Economic Review,* 6/18/76, 22.

UN response to the invasion

36 • UN voting. Arnold Kohen and JohnTaylor, *An Act of Genocide: Indonesia's Invasion of East Timor,* London: TAPOL, 1979, 38; Antonio Barbedo de Magalhaees, *Timor-Leste: Mensagem Aos Vivos,* LIMIAR (Porto, Brazil), 1983, 263–68.

36 • Ramos-Horta explains voting discrepancies. Ramos-Horta, 112.

37 • Roger Clark's analysis. Phone conversation between Professor Clark and author, 8/17/93.

37 • Moynihan quote. Daniel P. Moynihan (with Suzanne Weaver), *A Dangerous Place,* Little, Brown & Co., 1978, 247.

US support for Indonesia

37 • Bush on Iraqi invasion. Quoted in Noam Chomsky, "Nefarious Aggression," *Z Magazine,* 10/90, 19.

37–38 • Donald Keough quote. Quoted in *Dollars and Sense* (Somerville, MA), 5/92, 4.

38 • Cable from Australia's ambassador. Sun (Melbourne, Australia), 5/1/76, quoted in Kohen and Taylor, 34–35.

38 • Kissinger in Jakarta. Los Angeles Times, 12/7/75.

38 • US approval of invasion. Jack Anderson, "Another Slaughter," *San Francisco Chronicle,* 11/9/79, 61.

39 • US State Department condones invasion. Ross Waby, "Aid to Indonesia Doubled as US Shrugs off Timor," *The Australian,* 1/22/76.

39 • US trade with Dutch East Indies. Julie Southwood and Patrick Flanagan, *Indonesia: Law, Propaganda and Terror,* Zed Books, 1983, 22–23.

39 • Indonesia supplies 15 commodities. Jonathan Marshall, "Southeast Asia and US-Japan Relations: 1940–1941," *Pacific Research & World Empire Telegram,* 3–4/73, 7.

39 • Japan's defeat boon to US economy. US Congress, Naval Affairs, and Merchant Marine and Fisheries Committees, "No. 67: Survey of Pacific Areas," *Report to Chairman,* 5/29/46, 2, quoted in Peter Hayes, Lyuba Zarsky and Walden Bello, *American Lake: Nuclear Period in the Pacific,* Penguin, 1986, 20–21.

39–40 • Kennan's advice. George F. Kennan, "Review of Current Trends, US Foreign Policy," PPS/23, Top Secret. Included in *Foreign Relations of the United States, 1948,* vol. 1, part 2, Government Printing Office, 1976, 509–29.

40 • Nixon quotes. Peter Dale Scott, "Exporting Military-Economic Development: America and the Overthrow of Sukarno," in Malcolm Caldwell, ed., *Ten Years' Military Terror in Indonesia,* Bertrand Russell Peace Foundation for Spokesman Books (UK), 1975, 241; Richard M. Nixon, "Asia After Viet Nam," *Foreign Affairs,* 10/67, 111.

40 • US devastates Indochina. Noam Chomsky, *Turning the Tide: US Intervention in Central America and the Struggle for Peace,* South End, 1985, 216–17; Marilyn Young, *The Vietnam Wars 1945–1990,* Harper, 1991, 301–302.

40 • US supports Indonesian independence and curries favor with Indonesian army. Carmel Budiardjo, *Indonesia: Mass Extermination and the Consolidation of Authoritarian Power* in Alexander George, ed., *Western State Terrorism,* Cambridge (UK), Polity Press, 1991; Caldwell, 22.

41 • Suharto's slaughter, and US Embassy supplies names. Benedict Anderson and Ruth McVey, "What Happened in Indonesia," letter to the editor in *The New York Review,* 6/1/78, 42; Noam Chomsky, "'A Gleam of Light in Asia,'" *Z Magazine,* 9/90, 15–17.

41 • Suharto open to US investment. Carmel Budiardjo & Liem Soei Liong, *West Papua: The Obliteration of a People,* Surrey (UK), TAPOL, the Indonesian Human Rights Campaign, 1988, 33.

41 • US investment in Indonesia. Mark Selden, "American Global Enterprise and Asia," *Bulletin of Concerned Asian Scholars,* 4–6/ 75, 24.

41 • US companies supply 90% of weapons for invasion. Chomsky and Herman, 144–45.

42 • US military assistance. Arnold Kohen and Roberta Quance, "The Politics of Starvation," *Inquiry,* 2/18/90, 20–21; Taylor, 169.

42 • ABRI officers trained in US. Charles Scheiner, "No US Military Aid to Indonesia in Fiscal Year 1993!" *Bulletin of Concerned Asian Scholars,* 7–9/92, 51.

42 • State Department explains friendly relations with Indonesia. Waby.

42 • *Reporting on East Timor declines.* Chomsky and Herman; Taylor, 71.

42–43 • Los Angeles Times *reporting.* Matthew Jardine, "East Timor: Media Ignored Genocide," *Extra!,* 11–12/93.

Australian support for Indonesia

43 • *Hawke on Iraqi invasion.* Reuters, "Australian Warships Sail for Persian Gulf Amid Protests," dateline: Sydney, Australia, 8/13/90.

43 • *Fewer Timorese than Indonesians.* Quoted in Dunn, 141.

43–44 • *Woolcott cable to Canberra.* Bruce Juddery, "Envoy Puts Jakarta's View," *Canberra Times,* 1/16/76

44 • *Fraser undermines FRETILIN.* Kohen & Taylor, 105–7.

44 • *Australian military assistance.* Senate Standing Committee on Foreign Affairs and Defence of the Parliament of the Commonwealth of Australia, *Australia's Defence Co-operation with its Neighbours in the Asian-Pacific Region,* Australian Government Publishing Service, 1984.

44 • *Ford administration pressures Australia.* Michael Richardson, "Fraser given blunt warning at Washington talks: 'Don't anger Jakarta'—US protecting Indon channel for its N-subs," *The Age* (Melbourne), 8/3/76, 1.

45 • *Australian Defense Department paper.* J. R. Walsh & George Munster, *Documents on Australian Defence and Foreign Policy, 1968–1975,* J.R. Walsh and G. J. Munster (Hong Kong), 1980, 22.

45 • *Whitlam's foreign policy goal. National Times,* 7/19–24/76, quoted in Kohen & Taylor, 103.

45 • *Timor Gap oil field. TAPOL Bulletin,* 2/90, 18.

45 • *Woolcott's advice to Canberra.* Walsh & Munster, 197–200.

46 • *Portugal files case against Australia over Timor Gap.* Roger Clark, "Timor Gap: the Legality of the Treaty on the Zone of Cooperation in an Area Between the Indonesian Province of East Timor and Northern Australia," *Pace Yearbook of Internaional Law,* Vol. 4:69, 1992, 69–95.

Other supporters of Indonesia

46–47 • *Canadian aid to Indonesia.* Sharon Scharfe, *Complicity: Human Rights and Canadian Foreign Policy in the Case of East Timor,* forthcoming (10/95) from Black Rose Books, Montréal. Also her M.A. thesis in Legal Studies, Carleton University, Ottawa, Canada, 1994, *Blood on Their Hands: Human Rights in Canadian Foreign Policy?*

47 • *Canadian investment in Indonesia.* Department of Foreign Affairs and International Trade (Canadian government), *CanadExport,* 1995.

47 • *Canadian weapons in East Timor.* José Ramos-Horta, *Funu.*

47 • *Arms export permits.* Access to Information requests, 1995.

48 • *Japan second leading investor in Indonesia.* Selden, 24.

48 • *Japan leading investor in Indonesia.* Walden Bello, *People and Power in the Pacific: the Struggle for the Post-Cold War Order,* Pluto Press (London) , 1992, 84.

48 • *Japan leading aid-giver to Jakarta.* "Double Standard! Japan's Stand on East Timor," paper presented by the Free East Timor Japan Coalition to the UN World conference on Human Rights, 6/93, 2.

48 • *Japan's Diplomatic White Paper.* Quoted in Akihisa Matsuno, "Japan and the East Timor Issue: The Government, Citizens' Movement and Public Opinion," paper prepared for the 5th Symposium of Oporto University on East Timor, Portugal, 7/22–29/93, 2.

49 • *British ambassador's advice to Foreign Office.* Walsh & Munster, 192–93.

49 • *British assistance to Indonesia.* TAPOL, *Indonesia: The British Perspective,* 1993.

49–50 • *IGGI aid.* G.A. Posthumus, *The Inter Governmental Group on Indonesia (I.G.G.I.),* Rotterdam, Rotterdam Univ. Press, 1971; Budiardjo & Liem, 1988, 114; Taylor, 75–76.

Indonesia's war of occupation

50 • *ABRI limited to major towns.* Taylor, 70–71.

50 • *ABRI progresses slowly in rural areas.* Van Atta and Toohey, 6/6–12/82; Budiardjo & Liem, 1984, 23.

50 • *Indonesian casualties in first weeks of invasion.* "Jakarta's Timor Dead...," *Washington Post,* 1/9/76.

50 • *Four-month ABRI death toll.* Taylor, 70.

50–51 • *FRETILIN preparations and life in liberated areas.* Budiardjo & Liem, 1984, 57–59; Taylor, 70–71.

51 • *Encirclement and annihilation tactics.* Budiardjo & Liem, 1984, 27; Taylor, 85.

51–52 • *Lourenco's report.* Turner, 113–14.

52–53 • *Additional Western military sales and FALINTIL units surrender.* Taylor, 86–87; Budiardjo & Liem, 1984, 66.

53 • *Xavier's report.* Turner, 119–20.

53 • *Civilian deaths.* Taylor, 88.

53 • *FRETILIN's losses.* Budiardjo & Liem, 1984, 67.

54 • Relocation and deportation. Taylor, 85.

54 • Gusmao successfully reorganizes FRETILIN. Taylor, 115–16; Budiardjo & Liem, 1984, 67–69, 71.

54 • FRETILIN regains territory. Taylor, 115–16; Budiardjo & Liem, 1984, 68–71.

55 • da Costa's report. Turner, 185–86.

55 • "Fence of Legs". Taylor, 117–20.

56 • FRETILIN-ABRI cease-fire. Taylor, 136–37; Budiardjo & Liem, 1984, 72–73.

56 • Murdani breaks cease-fire. Sinar Harapan, 8/17/83, quoted in Taylor, 142.

56 • FRETILIN consolidates underground network. Budiardjo & Liem, 1984, 72–73, Taylor, 136–37.

56 • ABRI offensive and withdrawal. Budiardjo & Liem, 1984, 141–43; Taylor, 141–42, 160

56–57 • Military situation stalemated. Taylor, 160–61.

You're Indonesians, damn it!

57 • Military commander explains Indonesianization. Budiardjo & Liem, 1984, 98.

57–58 • ACFOA quote. Quoted in Kohen and Taylor, 88.

58 • Results of forced relocation. Taylor, 97.

58 • Forced labor in camps. Kohen and Taylor, 84–88.

58 • ABRI undermines traditional social organization. Taylor, 92–93.

58 • Babinsas. TAPOL Bulletin, No. 59, 1983.

59 • Justino describes resettlement villages. Turner, 178.

59 • Indonesia takes over former Portuguese enterprises and traditionally-held lands. Budiardjo & Liem, 1984, 106; Dr. Mubyarto and Dr. Loekaman Soetrisno et al., *East Timor: The Impact of Integration: an Indonesian Socio-Anthro-pological Study,* Indonesia Resources and Information Program (IRIP), 1991, 20; Turner, 193; Taylor, 123.

60 • Switch to Indonesian land tenure. "Timorese Convert to Indonesian Land Certificates," *Inside Indonesia,* 3/91.

60 • Monopoly lands with marines. Barry Wain, "Military Seen Behind Firm Controlling Timor's Coffee," *Asian Wall Street Journal,* 6/16/82, 1.

60 • Denok diversifies. Budiardjo & Liem, 1984, 106.

60 • Sandalwood monopoly. Wain, 3.

60 • PT Batara Indra. George J. Aditjondro. *In the Shadow of Mount Ramelau: The Impact of the Occupation of East Timor,* Lieden (The Netherlands), Indonesian Documen-tation and Information Centre, 1994, 58–62.

61 • *Indonesians replace ethnic-Chinese in economy.* Hadi M. Soesastro, "East Timor: Questions of Economic Viability." in Hal Hill, ed., *Unity and Diversity: Regional Economic Development in Indonesia since 1970,* Oxford Univ. Press, 1989, 215; Adam Kaye, "East Timor Depends on Jakarta's Largesse," *Far Eastern Economic Review,* 8/8/85, 20–23.

61 • *Local production replaced by Indonesian imports.* Taylor,127.

61 • *Anthropological study warning and follow-up.* Mubyarto et al., 51.

61 • *Schools emphasize things Indonesian.* Budiardjo & Liem, 1984, 111.

61–62 • *Physical education and* Pramuka. Taylor, 129; Budiardjo & Liem, 1984, 109–113.

62 • *Refugee testimony.* Quoted in Taylor, 128.

62 • *Indonesians increase schools.* Department of Information, *The Province of East Timor: Development in Progress,* Republic of Indonesia, 1980.

62 • *Illiteracy remains high.* Jakarta Post, 8/5/89, cited in Taylor, 129.

62 • *Birth control program.* Quoted in Taylor, 159.

62 • *Forced sterilization of women.* Taylor, 158; *TAPOL Bulletin,* 9/83, 8.

63 • *Belo denies population problem.* Asia Watch, 74.

63 • *Objectives and practices of transmigration.* Marcus Colchester, "The Struggle for Land—Tribal Peoples in the Face of the Transmigration Programme," *The Ecologist,* vol. 16, no. 2/3, 1986, 103; Taylor, 124; Aditjondro, 26.

63 • *Transmigration estimate.* Taylor, 124.

63 • *Transmigration target for 1992–93.* "For First Time, Central Java Transmigrates 25 Families to East Timor," 11/2/92, excerpted from an article in *Kedualatan Rakyat,* posted in reg.indonesia on PeaceNet.

64 • *25,000 heads of family migrate.* Anonymous, "Travelling in East Timor with Eyes and Ears Open," *Inside Indonesia,* 10/89, 25.

64 • *100,000 Indonesians in East Timor.* Xanana Gusmao & José Ramos-Horta, "Basic Questions, Straight Answers," *Aide-Memoire,* National Council of Maubere Resistance, 5/92.

64 • *East Timorese forced to join ABRI.* Dunn, 303–304; Budiardjo & Liem, 1984, Part II.

64 • *Jorge's story.* Turner, 172–74.

Recent developments

65 • *Expanding anticolonial movement.* TAPOL, "East Timor: Statement to the UN Decolonisation Committee—New York, July 1992," *Occasional Reports #19.*

65 • *ABRI hunts "two-faced" East Timorese.* TAPOL *Bulletin,* 2/93 & 4/93.

66 • *ABRI captures Xanana Gusmao.* TAPOL *Bulletin,* 12/92 and 2/93.

66–67 • *Ongoing resistance.* Matthew Jardine, "APEC, the United States & East Timor," *Z Magazine,* 1/95, 34–39.

67 • *CNRM founded.* TAPOL *Bulletin,* 4/90, 12.

67 • *FALINTIL's strength.* Stahl, 1994.

68 • *CCFD founded.* Joaquim T. Negreiros, "Timorese Resistance: I Conference Reinforces Unity," *O Publico* (Lisbon), 4/1/95.

East Timor's future

69 • *Gravel in our shoes.* Quoted in Jardine, 1992, 21.

69 • *East Timor not prosperous.* "Few Investors Take Up Invite to East Timor," *Australian Financial Review* (reprinted from *Asian Wall Street Journal*), 6/10/93.

69 • *ABRI casualties in East Timor.* TAPOL *Bulletin,* 6/88, 11; *Inside Indonesia,* 12/90, 8.

71 • *US arms sales continue.* US Department of State, Department of Defense and the Agency for International Development, *Congressional Presentation for Promoting Peace, Fiscal Year 1995;* US Department of State and the Defense Security Assistance Agency, *Congressional Presentation for Security Assistance Programs, Fiscal Year 1994,* US Government Printing Office.

My visit to East Timor

74 • *"Slaves of Indonesians."* Matthew Jardine, "The Secret Sacrifice of East Timor: Amid Invasion, Massacre, and Insurrection, the Church Takes a Stand," *Christianity & Crisis,* 2/1/93, 16–18.

76 • *The resistance has won politically.* Matthew Jardine, 1992, 21.

Recommended reading

78 • *Gaspar quote.* Jennifer Harbury, *Bridge of Courage: Life Stories of the Guatemalan Compañeros and Compañeras,* Common Courage Press (Monroe ME), 1994, 81.

If you liked this book,
check out some of our others:

The CIA's Greatest Hits   Mark Zepezauer
The CIA's many attempts to assassinate democracy all over the world are described in crisply written, two-page chapters, each accompanied by a cartoon. *95 pp. $6.*

Burma: The Next Killing Fields?   Alan Clements
Burma runs the risk of becoming another Cambodia. Written by one of the few Westerners to have ever lived there, this book tells the story vividly. *95 pp. $5.*
Deserves to be in every library. —Library Journal

The Greenpeace Guide to Anti-environmental Organizations   Carl Deal
A comprehensive guide to more than 50 industry front groups that masquerade as environmental organizations. The deception is amazing. *110 pp. $5.*
Fascinating. A must. —New Orleans Times-Picayune

Who Killed Martin Luther King?   Philip Melanson
This fascinating investigation of a murder that changed history shows why the official story—that James Earl Ray did it—just doesn't hold water. *94 pp. $5.*
Concise. Hard-hitting. —Oliver Stone

Who Killed Robert Kennedy?   Philip Melanson
This carefully researched book explains why Sirhan *couldn't* have killed RFK, and discusses who the actual murderers might have been. *94 pp. $5.*
Persuasive. —Publishers Weekly

Who Killed JFK?   Carl Oglesby
"I'm just the patsy," said Lee Harvey Oswald, and truer words were never spoken. This fact-filled guide tells you who really did what—and who didn't. *95 pp. $5.*
A must-have for all serious students of the assassination.
—Midwest Book Review